Book of the Highest Good: Volume 7

Open the Doors to Other Dimensions

By Joyce McCartney

Book of the Highest Good, Volume 7:

Open the Door to Other Dimensions

Cover Design by Adam Brown

Drawings are sketches by the author

Produced by Positive Options, Inc.

Print Version: ISBN-13-978-0-9863217-0-2

E-book Version: ISBN-13-978-0-9863217-1-9

Printed on demand by Amazon.com   First Edition, 2014

Kindle Version by Amazon.com First Edition, 2014

www.ingramcontent.com/pod-product-compliance
Lightning Source LLC
Chambersburg PA
CBHW071819090426
42737CB00012B/2136

Table of Contents

The Book of the Highest Good:
The Series

Book 1: A Beginning Experience

In this book, the author faces the universal experience of making sense of grief-filled reversal experiences in life and finds that she has two minds at work on the problem. One is the Conscious Mind of fear and regret, and the other is the Higher Mind of peace and love. Deciding to focus on the Higher Mind (calling it the Peaceful One) and ignoring the Conscious Mind (the Fearful One), she begins to ask questions about how life unfolds. She discovers that she is conversing with her Soul, which has the plan for her life and the resources to guide her in peace and happiness.

Book 2: Walk to Freedom

In this book, the author continues the conversation with the Peaceful One and finds out about the power of forgiveness and trust in the intention for the Highest Good. Once forgiveness is embraced, there is the opportunity to live in freedom to be happy. There is also a tantalizing look at how contact with one's Higher Mind can be used to solve practical problems of living one's life in peace, as a dialogue between two people each asking questions and channeling the answer from their Higher Minds, or Soul, is recorded.

Book 3: Being of Light

Once one can consistently contact the Higher Mind, one has access to vast amounts of benign and reliable information otherwise unknowable to the Conscious Mind. In this book, the author asks The Peaceful One about the health of the human body, the nature of the human aura, the workings of atoms, electricity, and the original creation of physical existence. Finally, an ancient pharaoh speaks, who begins to explain how the golden age of Egypt was founded upon the intention for the Highest Good.

Book 4: Channeled Tour of Ancient Egypt

The founding of the small town of mud huts that was later to become the mighty ancient Egyptian nation is described. It is essentially a story of a family, beginning with a mother who sets the founding intention of the Highest Good even before the birth of her son. With such a good foundation, the unfolding events show how the small boy could learn to levitate stones, cure the sick and injured, and advise rulers as to how to prosper their nations. We hear stories of everyday life and descriptions of the journey of the soul, which were later painted on under-ground walls. Finally, we have the nature of the Highest Good to be portrayed across the globe in a plan for peace in the modern age. This plan was left for us to find by the ancient Egyptians now reborn as modern citizens of peace.

Book 5: Stars Over Egypt

The question of extraterrestrial contact in ancient times is resolved in this book. The ancients had the Higher Mind to contact beings that congregate in spirit form on certain stars and planets, called the Hathors. Much technology and science was learned from these etheric beings. In order to understand this contact, the nature of a friendly relationship is discussed as well as the need to continually release fear, doubt, and regret. A clear channel only comes with a free and joyful outlook on life. Once contact with other dimensions is made, the good information gained can be put to use for the Plan for Peace.

Lastly a charming story of a lifetime of Edgar Cayce as RaTa is told illustrating how peace can be made in every transaction of life, even to the point of rejuvenation of the body.

Book 6: The Amarna Experience

The Egyptian town of Amarna was founded in the middle dynastic period in a previously unused site between two northern and southern, highly developed communities that had lost the belief in Maat. In this book, we are told the story of Akhenaten and his family who were not welcome in the north or the south as their ideas of the Highest Good, or Maat, were not in favor at the time. Thus Akhenaten leaves his family behind and finds a barren place in the desert to begin all over again to trust the Highest Good. Akhenaten learned to contact the star beings for help to find water, raise a crop, reconnect with his family, and to found a thriving, peaceful community that eventually seeded other civilizations all over the world with peace. As a model of how anyone can do the same today, this story lights a beacon of peace beyond no other to anyone who yearns to find peace, live in peace and give peace to others.

Book 7: Open the Door to Other Dimensions

If anyone ever wanted to know why the Earth is in the shape that it is, one only need look at the passageway between dimensions to see the conversations of peace coming and going. This passageway was used often in ancient times resulting in thousands of years of peace and prosperity. With the coming of Christ in His physical lifetime, there were more and better ways revealed for such inter-dimensional conversation. As Christ lives among us still, in the intentional double or etheric body, which accompanies all who espouse His teachings, we find that the old rules of the Highest Good still apply. Read along as the Grand Opening of the Great Pyramid is described and the placement of an intention for peaceful evolution on the Earth matures into modern times. If you follow this line of thought, you find yourself living in peace, health, prosperity, and happiness with all others.

Preface

If you had the opportunity to ask any question that you liked and then receive a wise and true answer, wouldn't it make sense to ask why and how the Earth was made the way that it was? Or maybe ask why do some people suffer while others do not? Why does one stay healthy while the other dies in pain? Once one has been around these topics for a little while, there is really only one question that has any meaning and that is: *Who is here with me to share this experience?* Whether the experience is life or death, who loves me, and I them, so much that we are here together? After all, isn't loving and being loved really the only essential element that makes one happy?

If one supposes that one is alone, then one is doomed to sorrow. If, however, one realizes that we are all part of a community of beings where all are together and never alone, then all are fated to be happy, no matter what happens in life. So let's take the second assumption for the premise of this book and never again wake in the night afraid or trembling alone in a storm. For never is there a place or a time when one can be disconnected from the Great Oneness unless a Conscious Mind believes it so.

With that as our premise, we must be about the issue of who all is there for us to have as our friends in this great community and how can we all get along. There are many places of interest in the etheric community and many who reside there, humans are only one type of being.

This book is about neighborhood introductions.

Let's explore where we are in relation to all others and who is in the neighborhood to love and be friends with. With that in mind, this Book and the following two (Book of the Highest Good, Volumes 8, and 9) discuss the idea of the etheric community in three vastly different ways. When the etheric community is completely understood, Dear Reader, you will see that there are many ways to exist, each inhabited by benign beings having unique gifts to give and receive. These gifts are so valuable that you will always want to be friends with your etheric neighbors.

Chapter One:
Meet the Family

Joyce: I begin this dialogue with the same name as before, but somewhat improved, for I am changed in a profound way. I cannot guarantee that I will sound the same as before, but let's try going forward together once again.

For once in my life, I feel that something has truly changed in my outlook on my life. It changed so much that my living alone is now seen as a blessing, which is sure to be followed by many more blessings later. How this all came about is not just the subject of this book. It is the nature of my experience to find peace all by myself, and then find so much more. I am glad to say that I am not the only one seeking peace. Indeed we are all part of a great community of peacemakers.

It has been a long journey of many years. With each experience, I gently and softly emerged from one solution of the mystery of life, to be confronted by yet another. At first, I thought that this was confusing and frustrating. I was sure that peace would never be mine. I returned, over and over again, to the task of releasing grief so that it would never again be found among my lost and lonely thoughts. But what happened next was to catch my breath in surprise. It was the final insight to put the Conscious Mind to rest.

I begin each story in much the same as it ends, on a sandy shore or in a sunny window, thinking about my life and my being. In the old days of grief, I would have regretted most of the deeds and events of my life, but not now. After all, they were the times of our lives. Just like a happy couple growing old together, I find that you, Peaceful One and Dear Readers, have been with me through all of it and graced me with some of the finest and richest of gifts. With each moment, we reacted to life with our private thoughts and feelings, wanting to make it better. We just didn't know how. We accepted much of it and laughed together. In the end, that was the relationship for which I had always yearned. Because it was an internal conversation, its nature was to be far more real and deep than any between two physical lovers no matter how true to each other they may be.

And now I come to the moment when I stand tall and proud to be *me* and find *me* to be good in all moments of my life. For without you, my beloved Peaceful One, I did have a problem with life. Now that my relationship with you is secure and constantly expanding, there is no hazard that we cannot handle together, but most importantly, there is no joy that we can't create. At this point, I can no longer imagine how desperate and frightened I was to think that I was on my own to struggle through life without the aid or support of your deep and powerful kindness.

I know that you are with me in life and in death and have been for a very long time. We will continue as long as we exist. How do I know that with such conviction when it was only a supposition just a few months ago? To answer that, I have to take Dear Reader on a journey started long ago and describe what I recently saw one night in a dream. It was a dream that I will never forget. I was looking up at the starry sky with no particular thoughts, when one star burst into a swirl of tiny lights, flowing round and round, coming toward me. I was startled and the dream ended, but I knew that it was something special. And now I ask the Peaceful One to explain the dream and to take us step by step on our long journey to the final insight.

As always, I ask for the Highest Good and nothing else. I remember the loving presence of the Peaceful One and feel gratitude and happy anticipation of the conversation. I ask for the wisdom of the dream.

Peaceful One: With such a long introduction, it only seems appropriate to say welcome home to my place of being.

For one to see that type of starburst as you saw in your dream is indeed a grand occasion. Many have come in search of it and never been granted such a view, as they must create many decisions of grief relief before even being able to approach it. What you have received is the passageway to being in the light even while in the dark.

Joyce: A passageway to being in the light even while in the dark. What does that mean?

Peaceful One: As an image, your dream showed an opening to spirit energy through which I came to be you and you came to be me once again. It is the portal, to and from the spiritual dimension. Being able to commune through the portal so easily, your dream would seem to say that you are me, and what is mine is yours and what is yours is mine. It was a sort of marriage ceremony. Not just a marriage of minds and hearts, this was a ceremony of two beings, which have been apart, reuniting in their natural unity of existence. Welcome to my world, which is a dimension different than your own, but just as real.

You are, indeed, holding your breath now. You have seen us meeting in space. Perhaps you are seeking to find a way to both experience and express what you have found to be true. This time it is really true, not just an idea. Shocking, isn't it, to see how truly grand it all is?

Joyce: Exhaling and then taking a deep breath. Passageway? Portal? Meeting together in space? Please tell me more.

Peaceful One: When you came into existence, there was only me and my spirit companions, but then I created you for a purposeful life in the physical plane and propelled you out of my dimension into that of the Earth. In doing so, you tumbled down the steps of consciousness, finally coming to rest on the lowest one where you found that you must be a stranger in a foreign land with no one to understand you. Do you remember thinking to yourself, as a small child, that this physical life is a dangerous place? A person could get hurt here, you thought.

Joyce: Yes, I was a very small child and I do remember thinking that very clearly. I was shocked that one could get hurt at all, but clearly one could. So what did that mean?

Peaceful One: What you saw at that time is the difference between the two dimensions, indeed the difference between the two minds that humans have. And all who were with you experienced the same conundrum. *How could I be a being of light and still feel alone and unforgiven for even the slightest of faults? In fact, what is a fault? I have no idea. I thought that I was loved all of the time for no reason at all. This place that I live within is very strange and not at all like where I came from. I'm not going to like it here. It is definitely not safe and I cannot find my other half anywhere.* Is that about the size of what you were thinking as a small child?

Joyce: Yes. It certainly is. I can recall that sense of loneliness being part of my whole life from that moment on. I never did resolve it or answer the question of my own existence. At least, I didn't until I started talking to you. Let me guess, you are my other half aren't you?

Peaceful One: How could I not be? We think alike, love each other through thick and thin, and find no joy when we are apart. Finding your other half is the most satisfying experience that anyone on the physical plane could have.

Joyce: Yes. It is a secure, familiar, safe, loving, and supportive feeling. It is the reunion with the better part of me, the part that knows the answers and has the power to make things better. No wonder I was so depressed when I was unaware of you. So why did we

11

ever part company in the first place? I'm not ever leaving you again, no matter what! I did not like that experience at all, so follow up the first answer with instructions so that we never part again.

Peaceful One: Why not always be together is the question at hand. Why not be free to be whatever one wants to be? Why not follow your companions to places that they wish to go, or even where they are (but would rather not be) and return with them in hand? Perhaps you have found that by writing these books that you have solved the problem for all others in the same predicament. Could it be that you and they are companions all in love with each other? Where they go, you must go. Would it be fair for Christ to come and make a bridge across forever without you being there to interpret it to millions two thousand years later? Would you have let Him down? Would you have let yourself down?

Joyce: Hold on there. You are implying that I came to help Christ. I would love to do that, but I don't remember making that promise.

Peaceful One: When you are in seeming demise, there is only one who can help and that is your other half. In terms of the history of the Earth, at the time of Christ, the Earth consciousness had been in decline so long that God, Himself, had to make way for another form of Himself. He wanted to create a way for humans to come back to the higher form of Himself – which is just like us, by the way.

    We are the many companions of Christ, as He has created us to be in perfect peace. We have many places to roam and to gain experience, but He looks after us at all times and in all places. For we are God's children and Christ is the child of His Father who made Him. Together, the Father and Christ guide all creatures on Earth. As those creations took form as humans, they lost control of the conscious connection to their spirit forms and thereby peace. That is why Christ asserted Himself into physical life to remind us of His great love for us and how to attain peace so that He could guide us back into His loving presence.

Thus He came and went, as did many others of his family. With some beings in distress and loneliness, the others came to assist and then found themselves in physical incarnation on Earth. All wanted a better life, but who would guide them? They prayed blindly for help. Help came over and over again with the Great Ones who taught truth and gave examples of a lifestyle that would allow them all to reunite with Christ. It is not like going home, for we occupy all of space, but rather it is a meeting of parts of oneself. Once firmly bound back together, there is no loneliness or distress, for life comes and goes as it should in a loving way, and we have no other way but that.

So once again, you have both stumbled onto your own solution and led the way for many others to do the same. You have followed the example of the Christ, the Master, as so many others have done, and graciously published your findings in a way that anyone can find them.

Joyce: Well, that sounds like a grand thing to do and, at the same time, a simple thing. To be that close to the

Christ Consciousness is a wondrous thing. I, and many others, would do anything to be part of His great heart. And although it will take me many pages to explain to Dear Reader what you just said, I know that exactly what you are saying is true. I know it because I saw the starburst opening and knew that you came to be with me and that I could go and be with you at any time, over and over again. So tell me more about the starburst spiral.

Peaceful One: The Earth was designed to be a place to make great decisions. The decisions are all about parting company, then choosing to reunite. With one wishing to be two, one must be initially distinct from the other, otherwise there would only be one. Thus, each projection of mind into new form, such as you were from me, needs to be given a set of experiences for it to be a self. It is much like a baby. The child is a separate person that comes to love and respect its parents so much that parents and child act in unison, each cooperating fully with the other. That is the stage at which we now function, as two beings cooperating as one and we do it as mind, heart, and spirit bodies operating in unison. And with that said, there is much grace as we cooperate and converse in an easy, natural way.

Indeed there is a life force transmission agent in charge of sending and receiving much energy across the dimensional membrane between spirit and physical life. Such energy and communication uses tubules or spirals of energy to make a passage from one to the other. Your starburst was one such tubule. The one that you saw in your dream was made by me to commune with you. Likewise, you make many to connect you to me such as you are doing to convey these words on this page. Now you can see that we commune whenever we want.

The fact that you saw and understood that it was I coming to you for a loving embrace is remarkable. If it had not been for the dream, you would have had to depend on the outside evidence over a long period of time – of good coming into your life as a result of our conversations – to convince you how near I am. With this being so, it is time for us to dispense with formalities and to begin to address the Earth with one mind and one message.

Joyce: I would have no problem with that. Since we are in strong communication and know each other to be open and friendly, we can cut to the chase so to speak. And we can do it on behalf of the whole Earth and all of its inhabitants. I think I just made a decision to be in your company all of the time, a decision that I will never regret.

Peaceful One: Then we have an agreement upon which we can depend. Let us continue to be one of mind, heart, and spirit body, letting all who know us see how big the peace project is in our mind and how awful it was to not be in peace. At last we have accord, indeed a very enjoyable event.

Joyce: You said mind, heart, and spirit body. I suspect that the part about spirit body is important, so please explain that a bit more. I think that I'm going to like this.

Peaceful One: If two were married, would they not blend their bodily needs and resources for the benefit of the other as well as for the emerging family? The new family would cohabit and live as one entity. I am proposing that we do the same and that you make me one of the happiest souls on record by saying yes to the question: Will you be mine?

Joyce: That is the finest proposal I've ever gotten and I accept. Yes, yes, and yes. I am saying yes to a spiritual being, but I have an idea that you mean more than just a mental reality. What is our spiritual family like?

Peaceful One: Would you enjoy being like Jesus when he walked the Earth? Would you enjoy being like Buddha when he blessed the Earth with his wisdom? How about the Virgin Mary and her many gifts of love? Would you like to be incorporated within them and function as they do?

Joyce: Yes, but I don't understand how that will happen.

Peaceful One: When one has had time as an Earth-bound soul to assess the situation and determine that improvement is necessary, then there are those of the higher kind who come to call. Would you like to be one of them and serve others who need to hear the calling to be in peace and to be taught how to do it? You could use your experience and your books that you have labored so long and hard to produce. Does that not sound like what you are currently doing?

Joyce: Yes, I must be on the right path. I do love to help others to understand what I've discovered. But I think I have an inkling of where else you are going with this. I remember the time that I was helping a family member recover from an illness and I was trying to help her, but it was starting to be at my expense. Then I hurt my foot and you said that only by curing myself, could I cure her. Conversely, by curing her, I will cure myself. Therefore, I can only say that when I do service for others that I will be curing the others and myself at the same time. I do the same as Christ and the saints did and I become one with them. How beautiful is that?

Peaceful One: How beautiful indeed. If one has a foot problem, does not the whole body respond to repair it? So it is with all brothers and sisters, even the family of spirit.

Joyce: I see. We are all one family and help each other. I have so many needs to be satisfied in order to be joyful all of the time. Now I understand that we are of one spirit body, mind, and heart and I now have full trust that my family will take care of my needs. I know that you will take care of all of my needs and thus the needs of all others. Because you are wiser, stronger, and more benign than my little Conscious Mind, you will have to lead the way. Because you know the way to be of service, we can fulfill our promise to Christ to help all beings to live in peace. I am in physical form so I can deliver the words and the presence of His kindness in concrete form to those in need. Because you are in spirit form, you will show the way. So where do we start?

Peaceful One: First is the question of where we are all to be found. When one part of you was in joy and the other a little sad now and again, we reminded you of an incident from your childhood. When you were a child lost in a crowd wanting to find your father, you looked up at the tops of heads. When you saw his black hair, you ran to him. Is that not the case even now? Do you not look for the higher part of each person that you meet these days? Even if they are in grief or disability and indeed being difficult to be with, you can always make contact with their Higher Minds and establish friendly and helpful contact. Would such contact not be as familiar and trustworthy as that of your father?

Joyce: I know what you mean. I often look at a person in great distress, who is being quite frustrating to deal with, and think of what their soul would be like. Then I see a mental image of the soul. I ask the soul for advice and their soul tells me what to do. I take it that you are saying that everyone is like this.

Peaceful One: Do you know me to be tried and true in my love and kindness for you? Have you known your father, mother, your sister and brothers, and now many friends to be the same? How have they all been in love with you either consciously or ethereally? Is it possible that they also have a spiral opening through which their Peaceful One comes to them and which they can share with you? Have you not interacted with the Great Oneness through such gifts of love from other people willing to give and receive love, even if clouded by grief and confusion?

Joyce: Yes, even the worst of personal experiences gave me something of you and I treasured that. In fact, I see all of us as good and ignore conscious intentions to deceive and use me. I accept that people can be mean and selfish, but even in those situations, no real harm occurred. Since I know them to be well connected to their souls as I am, I think that I will just ask their soul to send them so much love that they can't ever again be so cranky.

Peaceful One: Having said that, just how many of them have shown up, on time and in good order, to do as you needed, only leaving when the job was clearly on a good path?

Joyce: All of them. They came and went lovingly or rudely, but they did what was needed. And indeed, I need many more to come and love me and to help me with my project. I'll take lovingly rather than rudely, if you please. I suppose that is what this dialogue is all about.

Peaceful One: Then just call them: *Brothers and sisters come. I desire to complete my mission and to be happy in the process. I want your company.* There, now that is done and I assume that you will have no complaints in knowing that there are many more where they came from.

Joyce: Really? God must have created a really big family. Who else is there?

Peaceful One: How about the one who came and made you laugh and not cry anymore?

Joyce: Oh, that is my work buddy. He did make me laugh which made work much more fun while we both made a better living. So he was of my soul family. I guess that is why we got along so well.

This is interesting about being in families, some in spirit form and some in both spirit and physical form. I want to think about this for a while. This family idea helps me to see sprit beings and human beings as all related. Hmm.

Now that reminds me of another reference you made about the etheric double that every human has. So let me ask you another question about our family. How does an etheric double figure into this? How do we all communicate? Since we are all reincarnated family members, when will we all be one again and not separated? So many questions spinning around in my head! Time for a break.

Dear Reader, let's take a pause and start afresh on this topic of being a family. As usual, we must rest and give up any sad or grief filled thoughts and then come back to the dialogue from a higher view. It always works for us, so let's both take a few moments to rest. See you in the next chapter.

Chapter Two: Companionship

Peaceful One: When one comes to see a friend, whether for the first time or for the last time before seeing them in another form of existence, one wants to be addressed in the same manner as one intends to treat the other. Thus as a foundation of this part of our discussion, we must hear once again about the necessity of forming friendly relationships with the entire universe and all of the residents that live within it.

With this, we intend only the Highest Good for them, as well as for ourselves. And having forgiven ourselves for misunderstanding the benign nature of the universe, we do not doubt that it will be a loving and mutually beneficial relationship that may never end. Thus we find that getting comfortable is the first order of business. This process is much like an airplane passenger getting comfortable with the person in the seat beside them, knowing that it is a long trip and that much conversation will be needed to pass the time and to solve any problems that come along.

Knowing that all have a spiral access to their Peaceful One, let us not pronounce each other's name wrong or misjudge one's intentions. Once that has been accomplished, there are many places to go and see and many others to meet. Let's find a comfortable seat on the plane and know that our destination is the same as for all passengers: the Presence of God. Know that the terminal of departure is always crowded with people coming and going, even if only a few know the value of staying on course. It is for those who do, that we advise being at peace in mind and heart.

So with new places to see and new people to meet, let's not be sad to be saying goodbye to some of the ways of our accustomed thinking about the universe. Relax and loosen the seat belt of your belief systems and converse with the Peaceful One in the seat beside you about the gifts of existence and the problems of living life in both dimensions.

With the secure knowledge that all are Beloved Ones in search of other Beloved Ones for the sake of being Beloved Ones in love with their Loved One, we will depart shortly and may not return quite the same. It will be a pleasant trip — like a vacation – but just as any vacation does, this trip will change one's point of view. This trip will adjust your understanding to be able to speak the language of the Star Beings of Grace who have come to partake of the same gift of existence as you have, but who live in a different form.

+*+

Dear Reader, it is a clear day in May and the sun is shining. The warmth of the sun is giving birth to beautiful flowers and plants that give us food, beauty, and sustenance. While the winter was long and hard, life is easy and pleasant now. It makes me wonder about our existence in the Earth plane. Let's face it; sometimes life is wonderful and sometimes it's difficult and painful. After all, accidents, illness, and tragedies do happen. Sometimes we have good luck and sometimes we have great setbacks in life apparently for no reason.

Since the title of this book is: *Open the Doors to Other Dimensions*, I have to think that there is a lot more to learn about our existence that is unknowable to our Conscious Minds. Perhaps the Peaceful One will tell us more of how and why we exist and what is the purpose or goal. But even if I never come to understand it well, there's no one else that I'd rather be with than Peaceful One. Do you agree? I sincerely hope that you have formed an open portal to and from the Higher Dimension and are in perfect companionship with your Peaceful One.

Since I know that the universe is benign and life is a great blessing, I ask these questions on behalf of all of us who seek a better, higher understanding so that we can be peaceful and joyful at all times.

+*+

Joyce: Peaceful One, does existence in the physical plane always mean a mixture of what we would call good and bad events? Take, for example, the car accident that I had a year ago. It turned out fine, but it was a really scary experience. And while you are at it, why do these things happen?

Peaceful One: Why would one or two of life's events be about loss and setback, leaving one wanting more good? For if one had all that they wanted and wanted no more, then how and why would they be in love with love? Is not the human spirit a restless thing? Does not the hungry human heart tire of the same and seek a new sensation or experience? Humans move from one experience to the next seeking more love and then more still. To move from the lack of something to the fullness of it represents progress in a good direction. And so, to have something good removed implies that something much better must be coming. In short, you always move from good to better without any real harm. The question of what is real harm is a prevailing question that we have not yet completely addressed and therefore do so now. It is much to the question of why humans, even the well-intentioned ones, come to be in harm's way.

So let's begin with the end in mind. Where do we expect to be going when the end comes and we can evaluate the result of such mixed blessing journeys? With so many lifetimes, it must represent something very, very good. In order to explain the goal of physical existence, we must start from a different premise.

We would like to introduce you to the idea that there is, in fact, a cave of consciousness in which dwells One that always gives love and is, in fact, love itself. This Being is so compelling, that there is no entrance or exit sufficient in the cave as to entice one to leave, once entered.

Joyce: Cave of consciousness? Now you have really lost me. Is this a place or a state of mind or what? And, most of all, who is this wonderful Being residing there? I think I want to go there. How do I do that?

Peaceful One: Why not look in and see for yourself? All you need to do is to see me as a ball of light and then look through the center until it expands and yet another ball of light emerges and so forth until you find your destination. Since you are living within the aura of your soul, you can find me there. Since I am living within my Creator, you can go there as well. You can go on and on until you end in the Presence of God. Indeed we are partaking of a great journey from being a created one, to rejoining with our Creator. To do that, we pass through the portals of dimensions. You are going on that journey and will describe for Dear Reader what it is like to go back to our Creator through the long spiraling tube of light through which I am extending to be here with you, as you. And in doing so, I have opened the door for you to pass through to enter and explore me as you please. From there, it just gets more beautiful as we go from one benign being to the next.

Joyce: I am familiar with the tube of light. I've heard it sometimes called the silver cord. People who have near-death experiences see it as a tunnel of light. It runs between dimensions and I use it to channel, but you seem to be saying something beyond that. I have the feeling that it's not just words or thoughts that I will be getting. I have a feeling that it is a meeting of a being, a wonderful person in the cave of consciousness. Do I have that right?

Peaceful One: Yes.

Joyce: Hum! On the one hand I want to say, "let's go for it," but on the other hand, I want to ask more questions before we start.

Peaceful One: Why not do both?

Joyce: OK. Who will I meet?

Peaceful One: The me who is talking to you now is the first and then you will meet the me that made me what I am, and so on.

Joyce: So, we'll be following the trail of the Creators who created Creators?

Peaceful One: Each me will be one introducing you to the next, so to speak.

Joyce: That must mean that one who created another must be grander than the one created?

Peaceful One: That would be the case if you think "grander" is better than another form of "grand."

Joyce: So what do you mean?

Peaceful One: It is more like one *expanding* into another rather than one being grander than the other.

Joyce: Oh! So one Creator creates another version of itself by expanding. So both are the same, but one is in expanded form.

Peaceful One: Yes, and the purpose of these dialogues is for you to realize that this is a Oneness universe with unlimited variations. We are all related because we created or expanded one from another in bliss and joy.

Joyce: Well, it will take a whole book and maybe more to get that one straight, because it seems to be impossible to be One, but also different. Why are you taking me to this topic at this time?

Peaceful One: In order to be peaceful and happy and to understand the difficulties of physical life, you need to know where you are, what you are about, and why certain things do or do not happen for you.

Joyce: Yes, that is indeed a worthy exploration. Am I in a dangerous place full of disasters or am I inside a benign being getting to know the neighborhood? You are talking about feeling confident of one's own existence. After I have dealt with so many of my fears and grief, I guess we have come to the point of no return knowing that I always was truly peaceful, safe, and happy in life.

Oh, wait. I get it! You are taking me up another 10,000 feet to see life from a higher perspective and get much more out of the experience. As I rise in altitude, I get closer to the Wonderful One in the cave. And I know what comes next. The view from higher up gives more freedom from all fears and grief and thus lets in more joy.

And then…. And then…. I'm trying to absorb all of this. OK, I got it. As I go through life, I meet myself and others as higher beings looking at life from higher and higher up.

There is so much more to see that I can't even imagine while sitting on the ground any more. Well, that sounds like a great trip. Where do I get my ticket? Let's get on board and take off. Whoohoo!

Peaceful One: Well, then *where* do we start is no longer the question, but rather now we ask *who* do we start as. So let's start with the proposition that you are me and vice versa. I am your Higher Mind and you are in your Conscious Mind, but we live there together in peace. From the view of the Conscious Mind, there is an end of you in terms of the space that you occupy and the timeline from your birth to your passing over. Time and limitation gives a different world of meaning to the condition of being human in physical form. Assumptions of limitation, disaster, and death give so much grief. But these assumptions can only be held by the Conscious Mind, unaware that there is a limitless being (the Higher Mind) living in the same experience with it. The Higher Mind being cannot cease to exist and neither can the Conscious Mind, but it does change form. The thought of the loss of your physical "beingness" at the moment of death is a frightful thought. Have you ever really thought about that?

Joyce: Yes, actually, I have. Even as a little girl, I thought about what it was like to die and felt sad that my life and consciousness as myself would maybe end or change so substantially that the self that was thinking these thoughts would cease. It was too much to comprehend, so I stopped thinking about it.

Peaceful One: And that would be about where most people stop. But if one were a being of great strength, rather than the one so weak as to have an ending, would that being ever fear anything? Would that great being instead look to yet another version of herself for a greater understanding of who she is? Would not the Higher Mind maintain and support the lower? Being one, but existing in different versions, all versions would love all parts of themselves. I was with you as a little girl. As you were thinking fearsome thoughts about death, I was there helping and supporting you. You were not aware of me, but I was aware of you and loved you always, even beyond death. During the physical end, which is commonly called death, I will take you through a series of transitions so that we will always be together. So what are you thinking about now?

Joyce: That is very comforting to know. So why don't I see myself as being you? You are bigger and better than I. You are in a safe place where bad things don't ever happen, but I am in human existence where there are limitations and someday I will cease to exist as I am – at least as I see it.

Peaceful One: There is not a single problem with what you have said except the first statement about seeing yourself as being me? Would you like to take the first part of the trip and see me as I am, not as you *think* that I am? The first wonderful person that you will be meeting in the cave of consciousness is me. Aren't you glad?

Hello, madam, may I introduce myself?

Joyce (laughing): Yes, I am glad to meet you, for I know you pretty well, after all of these pages and pages of conversations. OK. I accept that you and I are one, or, at least, that we are friends. What do you want me to see about you that I don't already know?

Peaceful One: First, do you want me to be seen as your friend the cancer patient or rather as the golden ball of light above your own head?

Joyce: Now you have me going. How can you be both? By the way, I so love my friends who are facing their own healing and give them blessings as best that I can. So I love them. It could be me suffering from cancer and I don't want them to be alone or in pain. Oh, I see your point. I must be encountering you in them because all beings are one. But you are also an orb of light over my head as well as theirs. Dear Reader, get ready for this explanation. This should be good.

Peaceful One: How broad or wide of a definition of me can you allow me? Can I bring some happiness to a sick friend because you came to call? If I can do that for them, then I can do it for you when you need it. Can I be with you every minute in your mind and heart as you go your own way in life? Can I be the wind and the sun? Can I be the flowers and, yes, the annoying cat who keeps coming to your door and crying for company?

Joyce: Well, that would be a general concept of something very grand and big, not a person. However I know that you are a person not just an idea or concept.

Peaceful One: What kind of person am I that I cannot be whatever I want to be? Am I limited by your human definition of a person?

Joyce: Oh, I see. Of course, I have to go beyond my human mind definitions. Ok, well, let's see. How can I do that and still be human?

Peaceful One: There is no help needed, just let go of one idea of a form of beingness for a moment and let another take over. One form of you meets the other. One comes forward and speaks and the other listens, but both are completely you. How does that sound from where you are sitting?

Joyce: Well, if I imagine myself growing bigger and bigger like a balloon expanding to become an unlimited being in the form of light, then I can sort of get the idea. But where do I put the human me in this image?

Peaceful One: Right inside of the other. It is much like a turtle carrying eggs capable of growing into another version of mother turtle. In fact, she carries them for a very long time, before she deposits them in the hole she digs on the beach. In doing this, she is multiple beings in the form of one. We are just like that. I have been carrying you around inside of me for a very long time and then I gave you a brief experiential existence in time and space for the purpose of writing these books and so much more. However, the analogy stops there. You are in fact, still inside of me. You just carved out a little space to have your own human existence and I am supplying you with sustenance, friendship, guidance, and support.

Joyce: I'm inside of you? Then why did you say that you are an orb of golden light over my head?

Peaceful One: No one would believe the rest of the story until you came along, so we left the image as it was portrayed on the walls of Egyptian halls and tombs. It was a trail left to create more discoveries. But you, Great Mother, would not let your eggs lay dormant. You wanted another lifetime so that you could expand on the former thinking and bring it all back to just one central thought: One being within another being makes all beings one, living in safety and security.

Egyptian women generating spirals from an orb

Why do you think that the Highest Good works so well when it is applied to all equally? Is it not because if one has good, then all within that one must also have good or none will have it?

Joyce: Of course, nothing but a turtle can exist in a turtle and nothing but good can exist in a spirit being. We all exist inside spirit beings, so all is good. Wow. OK, it's time for a break. I have to think about this. Wow.

+*+

Dear Reader, I found this image of an orb in one of my Egyptian picture books. If the orb is a soul being, then the spiral coming out of it must be the openings created for many dialogues. I feel like the two women coming and going – mirror images of each other. Indeed my mind is stretching to understand this Oneness quality. If you get it before I do, send me some help. This is a big stretch for me. Let me ponder this for a day or so and then we can reconvene in the next chapter.

Chapter Three:
The Turtle or the Egg?

Joyce: As I am feeling my way through understanding this cave of consciousness, I find myself talking to others in spirit form and they are all one. I cannot talk to one without all of them hearing. When they respond, they all respond with one intention, but with many expressions. And so I am wondering about the idea of Oneness and find that it is a difficult concept to really understand. I went back to the reference to a turtle's eggs being turtle, but also independent. Then I am thinking that I am the egg living within Peaceful One like a turtle egg having a lifetime within its mother, but it must be one heck of an egg because it has physical sensations and interactions with others who are seemingly separate.

For example, I am thinking of a widow who is completely upset and in deep grief that her husband is no longer with her in physical form. She knows that she can contact him by etheric spirit.net, but that's not the same thing. He's not there talking to her, touching her, loving her, sharing in the work, the relationships, and the joys. So I understand your point about an entity having different forms, but physical form has its unique qualities and moving from physical to spirit form is one heck of a change. So please explain more about physical form versus spirit form.

Peaceful One: How peaceful could you be if you were so broken hearted to be without one that you love so dearly? Your friend's grief is to believe that they *could* be parted. How can there be joy in physical existence following such sorrow? Is that not your point?

Is it not the issue that the lifetime **seems** to come to an end, even though we leave for another place? Doesn't one seem separate and then, through long experiences of needing love and giving love, become one once again? When a mother has a child within herself, she must change the way she sees herself and form a new view of herself and the child. Just the same, when the child leaves the mother for its own life, a new view is also required. Her beloved changed form and she will be upset until she changes her view.

All physical existence occurs in time and space. Nothing is ever perfect, complete, or unchanged. To live in peace in this world, one must be willing to change one's view over and over again. It is one of the teachings of almost every religion that one cannot find God without being repentant of his or her old views of themselves and form a new one. Can you see that being perfect is not the purpose of life in the Earth experience? Physical form is temporal – trapped in time. And while such limitations apply, all things are essentially incomplete and constantly changing. While physical existence goes on, spiritual existence also goes on in peace and plenty, constantly expanding, and eagerly raising the consciousness of all little turtle eggs that happen to come along. As time unfolds, all come to be whole and intact with its Creator. This is quite a conundrum for the emotions and senses.

Actually the truth of the matter is that all temporal experiences are methods of coming back to oneness with you living within the one who created you along with all other selves who are also living there. Whether in peace or in conflict, all beings are still in the same place. They are all in a temporal experience where, no matter what they say or do, everything always changes.

"Get real and get happy" should be your motto. The reality of physical existence is that one can experience separation, but not be separate. Once you leave physical reality, you will see the truth. At that moment, there will be an immediate reunification with all who were living along side of you all of the time. And then we all know that we are all living within our Creator.

Now, have I clarified anything or just confused the confusion still further?

Joyce: I can sort of see what you are saying. We are all beings living within our parent – our Creator – and having a good time. Then, at some point, some of us take a partial view of ourselves, and step into an alternative temporal reality limited by time and space. Everyone else can see and experience it with us and even join us at the party, so to speak. Then, at another point, we stop looking at life in the partial manner. The time and space experience stops and we go back to being co-habitors within our Creator. It makes me think of a crystal that splits light into individual colors when just the right angle of light is present and that moment it produces a rainbow of color. The colors do not seem the same as the sunlight, but indeed colors are components of that light. Do I have it right?

Peaceful One: We are one step along the road. But why stop there? While we have you on the phone, so to speak, why not participate in a thought experiment? Suppose that you were a grain of sand living within a watery environment such as a stream. Then suppose that the stream picked you up with its strong current and deposited you somewhere else where you thrived and did good things as a grain of sand can do. Then the current picked you up again and deposited you in deeper water where you fell to the bottom never to see light for a long time. What would the grain of sand conclude about its dark existence?

Joyce: The grain of sand would think that it was in the dark and miss the light until it forgot all about the light and got used to the dark. Sort of sad, isn't it? Glad you said a grain of sand, not a person.

Peaceful One: Would that not be the same condition for many who come and go lifetime after lifetime without any knowledge of themselves as a small particle of a great rock so steady as to never be moved? The grain of sand was chipped away from the rock and has its own journey, but the parent rock stands the same. Part of the rock is dry in the sun and part is in the water, but nevertheless, the strength of the whole rock is such that it never moves. Now we have windy days and sunny days, hot days and cold days, but the rock stands and stands and never makes any movement. That is what faith in God is all about. You are part of God in all forms and conditions, including physical time and space where it looks dark and scary. But being part of God, you retain and enjoy the strength and power that He is, wherever you are.

Now, how can you walk in beauty, so to speak, when you are a grain of sand in the dark, wondering where the light is?

Joyce: Yes, that is how it feels. I recognize that I am a brilliant being, but where is the rest of it all? Why must I experience unhappiness at all?

Peaceful One: To understand that, you need to remember one of your best relationships. Do you not remember when you first met your favorite riding partner, a small quiet mule named Darla? Did you not think that she was made for you and you for her and that you would be together forever? Is this not the act of falling in love? Is it not this act of falling in love that so entrances you about any relationship? Indeed, it is the openness of the heart to be admitted without reservation that constitutes falling in love. And when you find this miracle to be your experience, do you not have a desire to have the joy of that miracle all of the time?

Joyce: Yes, oh yes.

Peaceful One: So inclusion is one and the same as being in love. And separation, rejection, and exclusion are of the most bitter of experiences. Is it not so?

Joyce: Yes, that is so. Those who suffer the death of their loved one find the seemingly final separation of death to be most painful even though it is not a rejection. I see my friend the widow struggle through each day wanting so badly to be in the physical presence of her Beloved One.

Peaceful One: Why should anyone include or exclude any being? If all beings are one, then either concept (inclusion and exclusion) is impossible. Even if a partner betrays his loved one and leaves with another, there is a missing of the time spent together. Where did they go that they couldn't be in love with each other and yet include the new one as well? Wouldn't that be more like the reality of the situation?

Joyce: Well, that would take a really big and open heart to accept that kind of thing. It is not part of our culture to accept such a thing that way, but I see what you are saying.

Peaceful One: While we are at it, let's take it one more step and say that one can never be just one individual. In fact, the universe is one great group experience. As the Long Story indicates, we are the Great Oneness and we experience what all others experience – nothing more or less. And with that one thought, let us see how and why one can feel loneliness at all. For that is the crux of the conversation.

If you and Darla were alone and having a good time in a barn or on a trail alone in the woods, would you not also be accompanied by the other beings present there as well? There are the flies, the beings of light living in light beams, the microbes, plants, and even manure beetles as the Egyptian used to write about. Although you are capable of being much more in love with those you perceive to be your equal or match, so to speak, these other small, innocent beings are present as well.

Joyce (laughing): Yes, you are right. But how do I have a relationship with a dung beetle?

Peaceful One: Perhaps they amuse you and make you laugh with their antics or possibly provide you with fertile soil for planting your beloved flowers. Enter into their environment and be with them, for they are lonely as well.

Joyce: What? The dung beetles are lonely? Now you are entertaining me and making me laugh. I have watched a lot of animals, especially birds, and I find that they are perfectly happy to go about their business, living and dying, as the day proceeds. They never experience the negative emotions that humans do.

Wait. Oh, I see what you are saying. The emotion of loneliness is entirely the making of the Conscious Mind. It doesn't exist outside of a confused and upset Conscious Mind. So you are saying that the dung beetles are happy moving manure around to do some good because they do not have Conscious Minds making themselves miserable about it. Maybe the dung beetle is smarter than me, after all. That is profound and funny at the same time.

In addition, I can see that every speck of conscious life showed up to share a moment in time with me. We all shared the experience and are therefore all one.

Egyptian dung beetle

Peaceful One: To follow this logic, the Conscious Mind decides to include or to exclude one or the other of life experiences small beings of light, or even people. Once the idea of inclusion and exclusion is accepted, then the rest of the misery plays out. Take the fine art of making judgments about another. Does that not separate one from another?

Joyce: Now I am thinking of how the whole idea of human marriage is built upon some of these assumptions. When a couple meet and determine that they are acceptable to each other, they include each other into their most intimate life experiences and the inclusion feels like Heaven, which it is. Then they come to find some things that they don't like about the other and they have to choose to include or exclude all or part of their Beloved. By continuing to include, they open their hearts and Conscious Minds and stay in their experience of Heaven. If they exclude the other, then they experience exclusion and all of the negative emotions that go along with that false belief.

Peaceful One: Once again, the Conscious Mind is not doing a very good job of portraying life as it really is. It is just too small and undeveloped to see reality correctly. And to make it worse, the Conscious Mind creates the fear that once death occurs, that the mind ceases to exist and thus the individual as well. It completely ignores the existence of the Higher Mind and all of the other beings alive and giving love in the universe.

The fact that a marriage has a start and an end tells all. It is temporal and, thus, passing in and out of one existence and then another. Think of life as a temporary extension of Higher Mind for the purpose of experiencing both lack and abundance of good things. When the time comes for another experience, the Conscious Mind is retracted or reaccepted into the Higher Mind, complete with all of its memories, emotions, experiences, and knowledge. Therefore, if one has lived many lifetimes, done many projects, and had many marriages and relationships, what do you think happens to all of those Conscious Minds?

Joyce: I guess they all reassemble within the Higher Mind and live and grow there. They are the children of the Higher Mind and therefore can't stop existing. The only movement in the universe is outward for new experiences and then inward back to God. So if I've had a thousand lifetimes, then I have a thousand Conscious Minds? Is that true?

Peaceful One: How could one have many minds with which to think and to live? How about many experiences enjoyed by an expanded mind? The choice to use a mind at all is much like picking a pear to eat. Which one is the best fruit for the day? Which shall I leave for another day? The Higher Mind is capable of being in love with each of them individually and all of them all at once.

So would you like an example of several Conscious Minds in play so to speak? How about your lifetime as Edgar Cayce and then the one as his spouse as well as her sister and their sons? If we are all one, then you were all of them and the record of their minds is the record of all of our lives. Could you indeed be among the many who have been on a very long path to be the makers of peace upon the Earth? And if all are one, then there is no one who can be separate or excluded. Being included is a forgone and permanent condition. Thus no one is alone or could possibly be alone, so no need to feel lonely or unloved.

Joyce: Now that you have taken me round and round that thought, I'm not sure just *who* I am. I guess that is the point. I don't have to be just one individual. I am part of all others and all of their experiences, so indeed no need to feel lonely. And even if I do feel lonely, it is just a Conscious Mind misunderstanding. It is certainly not real.

In many ways this is an astounding statement and it changes everything about how we see ourselves. I would like to spend a day using the pronoun "we" instead of "I" just to get a feel for our true reality.

+*+

Dear Reader, we are truly we. I knew it from the start, didn't you? Why else would we all be here at this time and place experiencing all of this together? I can remember all of your experiences and you can remember mine. We can know, understand, and help each other, if we choose to try to see things as Oneness. What if the whole population of the Earth did that? Just how quickly would the resources be equaled out and peace settle in every part of the world? Well, we can see why Peaceful One has been talking to us about this topic. Give it a day or two and say "we" when you want to say "I." See what it does to your world. After that dust settles, read on. I have a feeling that there is much more to find in this cave of consciousness.

Chapter Four:
Make Mine a Double

Joyce: I have been sitting by the firelight in this cave of consciousness visiting with Peaceful One for two chapters when, suddenly, I see a shadow on the wall. It is a shadow made by the fire, but there's no one beside me to cast the shadow. It moves and talks on its own. It is saying wonderful things and makes me feel at peace.

Peaceful One: Now you have found this cave to be a place of many wonderful beings. Get comfortable and I will introduce you to an etheric double – one that is quite famous, in fact.

Joyce: This is one more issue that I still don't understand: The making of a double. What does it mean to have a double or to be a double? What do they do? How do they exist? Well, you know all of the questions that I want to ask. Please explain more.

Peaceful One: Your mental self can have as many forms of itself as it wants, but the physical one can only be itself. Therefore, if your soul wishes to form another version of itself – even having the appearance of the physical form – it can. This is why it is called a double. As an offspring of the soul, it can even act upon physical matter in the same way that a soul can. But with that said, it is not temporal and thus does not have a beginning or an ending. It is essentially a solidification of the soul's intentions and once that it has been made, it continues on and makes many others. You may think of a double as a fine feathery web extension of a soul that can be extended and then drawn back into the soul.

For example, while you were in Florida on a family visit, you had a double in your home city, performing grief relief, and another double at the farm doing farm things. You would see them as fine shadows floating about and feel them as shivers or temperature changes on your skin if you were in their presence. The idea of a ghost is an interesting comparison, but a doubled being is a part of a soul and is always benign, never lost, and easily communicated with. Some people take photos in low light and see white orbs floating around certain places. These are etheric doubles condensed enough to reflect light for the benefit of the camera lens. A double condenses and becomes visible in this way when the intention to do a particular good is intensified. Therefore, they are frequently seen around great monuments of peace. Do not be afraid of them as they are always sent on a mission of peace and goodwill. When they have completed their task, they return to the soul that projected them.

Although Christ in physical form no longer walks the Earth, there are many doubles of Him in etheric form. He doubled and redoubled himself over and over again to form a new foundation for peace upon the

Earth. Does that surprise you? Did you know that He roams the Earth in etheric form doing things of grace everyday in many places all at once? He's even come to your farm to deliver things to your door as a deliveryman.

Joyce: What? You have a way of entertaining and teaching at the same time and I love that about you, but how can a deliveryman be an etheric double, especially of Christ?

Peaceful One: Glad to see a smile on your aura. You are trying too hard to understand this. I am saying that his etheric double acts upon all parcels delivered to you. He gives you peace with each delivery because he is a good man and intends peace in every part of his life. His soul created a double of himself and uses it to impart good on his job. It is an intense intention turned into an intentional energy being. It even looks like him. It does not look like an orb.

You do the same when you work at the foundry. You use your double to further explain to the workers what your meaning is when you counsel them. You do this because it is hard for them to understand at first. The double stays with them until they learn what you have intended for them. When they remember you, the double continues to teach them even after you have left. They just think of you and they get the instructions you intended for them to understand. Thus you are a physical person using an etheric double to perform the mission that Christ initiated. Thus in this sense, you are the etheric form of Christ. In Egypt, it was known as the

Ba mentality. It was consciously used and appreciated then and it is about to be used again today.

Joyce: Yes, I remember references to the Ka and the Ba. They were depicted as little birds that could fly, but had the head of a person. So what did we use them for in Egypt?

Egyptian Ba leaving a body to complete a task

Peaceful One: To do good deeds, of course. That is their only use. For example, if we needed someone to accompany a friend on a long journey, their family would send their Ba as a companion to help and assist with the travel. If one saw a mysterious traveler coming in the direction of the town from a great distance, they would send their Ba skyward to travel to see and investigate who it was and then return to tell the tale. If one wanted to travel to another universe or dimension, one would send one's Ba. *Hint, hint,* one could always do that to go through the portal between our dimensions.

Joyce: You mean that this is how I am receiving these readings and that is how inter-dimensional "travel" happens? This sounds pretty important to me. Let's explore it further not only for me, but also for all Dear Readers who will be trying to do the same.

Would you describe more about using one's Ba? Let's start with a good name for our semi-physical selves.

Peaceful One: Since you have given me a fine name that befits my nature, let's do the same for our fine semi-physical self. Let's call the Ba, Enlightened One. Now let's consider that Enlightened One's nature is to be light, thus it can travel where light or any vibration can go and return unharmed and transmit the information acquired by digital download.

Joyce: Wait. What? Digital download?

Peaceful One: With such a shocking reference to computer technology, we must explain a bit more about computer chips and the flow of information.

Just like a chip of crystal organizes the flow of electricity into on and off passageways in a computer, our Intention for the Highest Good allows only the good to be on and leaves no opening for bad. Consider a mind (any mind with such an intention) to be like a computer chip capable of processing good in varied forms and never any bad. As Enlightened Ones, we move around the universe unfettered by physical constraints and can find good wherever we need it and bring it to the attention of a similarly programmed Conscious Mind.

Can you now see that a Conscious Mind that admits that it can receive bad is not a good receiver of

Higher Mind? The realm of Higher Mind cannot choose whether to be good or bad. We can only choose what kind of good to be. The human Conscious Mind does have the choice of good or bad, thus if it is a conductor of bad, it cannot receive much good. Once one has the intention for good, however, then all bad is disallowed and only incoming downloads of good can be received from the realm of the Higher Mind. That is why you are such a good reader of Higher Mind. Long ago you decided to engage in good and no bad. It was a momentous decision, as you can now see.

Joyce: Yes, I see that now and I am glad that I made that decision. But let me comment that this is also another way to explain the power of forgiveness. The on/off switch of our intentions is a powerful part of human nature and it totally determines our happiness or our grief. In the book, *Being of Light*, you clearly told us that the intention for the Highest Good opens our chakras and allows the healing energy of the soul to replenish the body, thus protecting it from illness and decline. Here we have another opportunity to know the consequences of a decision to not allow any bad to be a part of us. If we allow only good and no fear, judgment, or doubt, then we have all good. If we allow that any harm could come to us, then we receive mixed signals. If doubt is extensive enough, we don't match the program of the universe enough to get much of anything at all. We will get the error message that the download failed, try again later. It would be very confusing – a little good and a little bad all mixed together. No wonder people have a hard time with spirituality.

I understand that connecting with the good of the universe is all within the choices of our minds and hearts. Outside of the fear of our Conscious Minds, the physical natural world is all good and our life plan is all good, even if it contains some apparent challenges. I am beginning to see that if we align our Conscious Minds with the decision to have only good, that we make a connection between the spiritual reality of good and the physical reality of good by removing all mental fear and doubt. We would be a conductor, rather than a resistor of good. I'd think that good downloaded from the universe would release a lot of energy. It would be like plugging into a wall outlet and seeing the lights go on.

Peaceful One: At this point, don't you wonder what your Enlightened One (Ba, Etheric Double) is thinking? Since we are all one in spirit, let's address Enlightened One as plural, if you can stand the irony of "One" being plural. If not, think of One as referring to Oneness.

Joyce: The fact that your ironic statement makes perfect sense to me either means that I am significantly more wise these days or I have lost my old mind and acquired a newer, more spiritual one.

Peaceful One: Maybe both. Maybe if I were going to draw a picture of your new mind, I'd draw your form with the head of another being such as Anubis, the dog who tracks down its satisfying dinner without fail, or maybe Horus the hawk, who views the world gliding on a higher stream of air and only comes down to find a meal.

Joyce: Oh, I see. You are saying that the ancient Egyptians already knew all of this and drew themselves on the tomb walls as a record for us to verify that we are doing the same sort of thing today. If it worked for them, it will work for us.

Annubis the Dog and Horus the Hawk

So, Enlightened One, welcome! I know you have been with me for so long that I can hardly tell the difference between us, but I would like to have conscious communication. Would you speak about our relationship and how we can do good together?

Enlightened One: When one has reached this point in the transmission, there should be nothing to intervene between those who wish to work together so closely. I know that there has been a hiatus of almost everything else that would be distracting in your life, but do not think that your aloneness will lead to your demise. None who makes this transition into this type of contact ever has a need to be concerned about any resource or how to do anything. We Enlightened Ones do everything in easy mode. Thus we find that being enlightened, we are on the job all of the time. Come to think of it, "gracious and generous" is a good definition of our relationship.

Joyce: How nice to hear from you and to see that so much that is easy and good is ahead for us. Please continue.

Enlightened One: When one has made such a connection between the Higher Realms and the Earth, there is indeed a great release of energy, which is what happened when the Great Pyramid was commissioned, causing the ground to tremble. No harm was done as it is all for a peaceful purpose. But for the purpose of our discussion, let's look closer at the need for spiritual star beings to be participants in our ever-expanding family of minds all in tune with the same intention.

As guardians of the Earth, there are indeed several star beings of etheric form that have explored many different ways to enhance the peaceful flow of energy in the Earth's magnetic field. They wish to propose at this time how to salvage what is good about what is going on in the world today and discard the bad. Therefore, let me travel to their place of residence in the star system, Arcturus, and bring back a message of peaceful co-existence for all men who dwell on our beautiful planet.

Joyce: Arcturus? I think that Peaceful One told me that most humans go there after death for part of their sojourn (experiences between lifetimes). It must be populated with many who have lived upon the Earth and seen its needs from the ground as well as from the spirit side. So, yes, I can see how this would be a worthy trek.

Guardians of the Earth: We are not all Arcturians, as we represent the interests of many places in the galaxies. But be sure of our need to be in contact with each other and indeed you. For you have volunteered to give us a

52

voice comprehensible to modern society so that mankind living upon the Earth can cooperate with the benign plan for a peaceful planet. There is literally nothing bad that can come between us.

In enlightened existence, there is no time and it is for us to tell all readers of this book that there are many of us who are lined up waiting to do much good for the Earth. We wait for the scientists and environmentalists to inquire about how to do some good, rather than wishing for some prophecy of doom. In saying this, do not think that the knowledge we wish to give is esoteric. We would offer some very simple suggestions at first, and later to offer more complex ones.

For example, there are some general approaches in lifestyle changes that will so further all life upon the Earth that all will be amazed. Should every human avoid flushing one toilet a day, the flow of pure and clean water could continue forever. Should environmental laws prohibit the fishing of waterways beyond a reasonable limit, the fish would prosper and further clean the water. Indeed, this is being done to some extent. We always start with the simple suggestions that give the best results.

Furthermore, when one wants a good clean drink of water, one should receive it with appreciation and seek to define it as a resource to be preserved, managed, and appreciated. Know that there are orbs of light in every drop of water. They live there in grace. Allow them to live there in peace, applying no other ingredient, and merely filter water in an efficient way. Many suggestions for better disposal of waste and sewage will be discussed with anyone who inquires with a pure interest in good information for the purpose of peace.

Thus we have given an immediate example of how easy and good a trip to the nearest space station of peace can be. Indeed some of us are "self-cestors" (souls who have lived as humans before and have returned). We have experienced all of this before and are eager to repeat the good learned from the past.

Joyce: This seems a lot like what I have learned in other readings. I realize that there is no time in spirit realms, so it does not take any time to accomplish this transmission. And I realize that we are all deeply familiar with all of this ancient knowledge, but what, exactly, was the contribution of Enlightened One?

Guardians of the Earth: When one needs the best advice, one goes to those who have it to give. Thus consider the etheric double, now known as Enlightened One, as the finder of the best advisors and the maker of the necessary connections. Being spirit – an orb of light – not in a human form, Enlightened One can pass through solid objects and travel instantaneously anywhere without any loss of energy. Thus it is quite efficient to contact and use us. Think of it as the Enlightened One providing a way of holding an enormous conference call with the greatest minds in the universe on many different subjects.

Indeed we would like to suggest that those in charge of professional conferences where good questions could be asked think to invite us as well. They can call the meetings the "Greatest Minds on

Environment Topics." Such conferences could address medical, archeological, scientific, social issues, or, indeed, on any area of interest. Once such a meeting is thought of and arranged on the physical level, preferably in a natural place rich in peacefulness, then the Greatest Minds of the Spiritual Universe will arrive on time and be ready to attend as well. Should all physical participants be channelers with Enlightened Ones ready to act in spirit form and well tuned to the job, so much good could be accomplished that none would leave disappointed. By means of such conferences, the calming of the Earth's magnetic fields was accomplished many times in ancient times and will be done again.

Joyce: So you are suggesting that professional conferences on certain topics be conducted with channeled information being supplied from the Spirit Community. This is a wonderful way to get the highest collaboration focused on a problem. It would create good in a delightful manner. The term Greatest Minds is a good one. I can see an image in my mind of a huge conglomerate of individual minds working as a single mind with a single purpose. No telling what we could accomplish with this type of mind power.

Now, at the end of the last paragraph, you mentioned the calming of the Earth's magnetic field. That sounds pretty important. Would you say more about that?

Guardians of the Earth: When one has a cold or trouble breathing, one has the urge to sneeze. This is just what the Earth does once in awhile. The sneeze consists of land upheavals, wind, and rain associated with great storms. While this can be cataclysmic in terms of human civilization, it is completely natural. But the conscious collaboration of many focused on preventing such events is also quite naturally beneficial. In the past there were meetings of Great Minds on such matters which led to very long times of peaceful life on the Earth.

If conferences such as this were conducted, there would never be a need for polar shifts of axis as Cayce described. In fact, he hoped to prevent the shifts by making people aware of the fact that his ability was normal and available to everyone. Living on this planet could be quite blissful indeed if needed information could be transferred across the dimensional barrier. Thus we end this part of our discussion describing the existence of Enlightened One. It would be wise to get acquainted and very comfortable in order to make a good working team. We stand ready, willing, and able to do what a Conscious Mind cannot do.

Joyce: Am I glad that I welcomed you and decided to channel your messages! This has opened so many more doors of opportunity for the Earth to exist in peace. Thank you so much.

Enlightened One: Now that you have realized that there are doors between dimensions that need opening, why not include a drawing of the ancient Egyptians' depiction of a door opener just like me. Notice that these statues were always placed somewhere where light could reach them.

Enlightened One in a doorway

Joyce: This is a beautiful work of art, but I am glad to understand its significance. I take it that the figure in the doorway is an Enlightened One coming and going, so to speak. I think that I will put a more modern version of the cave of consciousness on the front cover of this book.

But one last thought. I am still thinking that when there is a connection between the dimensions, there is a release, or maybe better said, connection of great amounts of energy.

Enlightened One: You have been feeling this energy for quite some time as peaceful flows of bliss. As more of this type of energy is shared, it is less likely that the natural disasters need to occur. Thus even though Great Minds are meeting to discuss specifics, all human participants should sit quietly, wherever they are, and connect to their Higher Minds with the intention that the Earth be at peace. How many minds making connection does it take or how long? Not much to be said there except that it is not long at all.

Joyce: That is interesting. I can see how this connection thing all works. Thanks, Enlightened One. I suspect, however, that there are other services that an Enlightened One would love to do.

Enlightened One: The use of a Ba is entirely determined by the soul using it. There are no limitations, except that it could only be used for the Highest Good. Indeed one needs to be totally dedicated to the Highest Good to use it at all, for it cannot be used for harm or for lightly held reasons. There must be a true need for it, a good intention, and the will to sustain its activities in cooperation with the Higher Plane. It is indeed a participant in the interrelationship between the Conscious Mind and the Higher Mind and a member in good standing in the Great Oneness. But to answer your question, the Enlightened One (Ba or Etheric Double) loves to heal just about everything and everybody.

Joyce: So you say that you made one for me to use for my work with supervisors who come to my training. How else has it been used and why?

Enlightened One: Anyone who has direct access to the thoughts of their Peaceful One is entirely able to make and use their Etheric Double. In fact, it is your Enlightened One who translates the vibrations of Higher Mind into your familiar form of speech for you so you can do the readings.

As a Ba, I am in favor of the Highest Good at all times and places and nothing else. I have appeared to you as The Blue Lady, completing your healing requests, but I am really a fuzzy ball of light snapping with energy. There is no gender, only a strong intention for good in the form of a being of light.

The Blue Lady

We can accomplish any peaceful request promptly with no effort on your part. For example, last night you requested that your hair be restored to your natural color, a request that I was glad to do for you. Because you are a restorer of peoples' faith in the existence of the benign world, you need to look well cared for. Therefore, I will perform a nightly ritual emitted from your crown chakra that will make all of your hair follicles respond to light energy and slowly return the hair to its natural color of golden brown.

Joyce: Thank you. It's like having my own personal hairdresser, only with no bottles of hair color or hair dryers. By the way, why the image of the Blue Lady? Why not some other image?

Enlightened One: Would it surprise you to know that this image is one with which you are very familiar, having used it over and over again in many lifetimes. Actually it originated in the images that you saw in the waters of the Nile River during a night boat ride. You thought that you saw yourself, but it was too formless to be sure. The stars were twinkling on the surface of the waters. It seemed so right to you that you took it as your image of me and I agreed to perform under that image. You have been using it for the purpose of healing for millennia and it has worked quite well. We are old teammates and work well together.

A more obvious incidence of my help occurred last year. If you ever had any doubt as to the effectiveness of your Ba, your car accident of last year is the best evidence. Your car was completely disabled, but you walked away with no harm at all. If the good outcome was caused by the fact that you were belted into a well-designed and crash-tested late model car, then you would be content. But lately, you have been hearing from us that damage control within your internal organs was the true gift of that car accident. Because it was not your time to depart physical existence, I automatically stepped in to cushion your internal organs, nerves, bones, and joints in order to preserve your body in tact

60

for more Highest Good to come. Without this intervention, in most cases of impact accidents, there are little bruises, tears, and inflammations that are caused by the internal effects of such a crash. For you to just walk away with no damage other than being a little shaken emotionally is truly a miracle and a testament of my existence.

Now let me tell you another story of your existence, which I have saved just for this moment. Do you remember when you were a little girl that the last thing at night before you fell asleep was to talk to God under your covers? I was the one who brought God's answers. I made your little girl's heart feel at ease. Did you not have many dreams of flying? Were you just like those Egyptian birds with human heads? Those dreams were of me coming back to you with many images of grace and a feeling of how much help you have available. I was confirming how beloved you are. There is not much else that I need to say for I see that you are now convinced, so let's proceed with the second request which is to define how to use your Enlightened One now.

If you were to pick up a powerful tool such as a power cordless drill and use it effectively, you would need a plan for its use. You would assemble the various parts and recharge the tool so that it is ready for use. This is much the same for what we have to do to be good work companions once again. So let me begin at the beginning and make such a plan.

As you said in the Long Story, in the beginning there was God and God was good and happiness itself.

Then God decided to create souls, for whom happiness would be His gift. Their gift to God would be to reciprocate that love both among themselves and God. Thus in saying these words, there is an implied contract that it pleases God to make you happy and it makes you happy to love God back. Consider us doing that in all things that we do together. We are limitless beings in love with a limitless being. Together we are all high flyers in need of others to love.

Joyce: Well said and thank you, by the way, for saving my body's functioning during that crash. It illustrates how powerful you are to be able to accomplish such a thing even if I was not aware of it.

Enlightened One: Thank you for giving me your appreciation. Appreciation allows the grace of existence in the Presence of God to continue on with the giving of much good. It was much more than my saving your body from harm. That is just what I mean about reciprocating love. We love to be appreciated and to have our efforts be used for the good of all beings. Thus we have now consciously made a contract to love and care for each other henceforth. Now we need a plan for the rest of your life.

Because you are a being of light that gives only grace, you will be requiring much rest and the recharging of your life energy. Thus there is no time to be spent on second-hand relationships that do not return love in kind. Only reciprocal relationships given by the best and most beautiful ones who consistently and positively love and support you will do. With this in place, there is little else that you will need, but the appreciation of the events of the moment as you proceed with your writing, teaching, and giving of grace wherever you go.

So do not think that our relationship has a long way to go or takes a long time. Indeed our relationship is always available and is as close as your own thoughts. If you will determine with me that the best – and only the best – will do, then I will proceed with the plan for your lifetime. We do have wonderful plans to manifest, don't we?

Joyce: Yes, we do. I want nothing less than the best. So with that in mind, how would we proceed? I would like to be consciously aware of our work, as it will generate much appreciation, which I know would please you as well.

Enlightened One: How fond of you I am. Yes, I have been helping you all along, but it would be a pleasure for us to consciously share the many good things that I can bring to you each day. Thus, let's have an agreement that, once an intention is set, I will take care of it completely. We can also discuss the progress of the work and enjoy the many occasions of giving and receiving of love. Just for fun, I'll give you a recap of what transpired last night.

Joyce: Oh, good. I knew that something was happening last night and I had a guess about what it was. I want to hear it from you.

Enlightened One: Well, we took a look at the whereabouts of the man graced with helping you with your books and found that he was a great one in charge of much book production and could currently be found in Paris, France, at a book conference regarding the benefits of e-publishing for independent authors. Then we touched the place in his heart where you were to be found and he opened to us being there in peace. Then we transferred a thought or two about your need to be in retreat a while longer, but implied that there would be a meeting as soon as it was feasible.

We agreed to be consciously in touch with him as well, telling him all about you and your work. Thus with the seeds of transference in place, there was no harm done for either and much good. Now be about your business and he will be about his. When the time comes, both will be in place, willing and able to proceed, for his Ba and I are in complete cooperation, as will be the Conscious Minds of each person involved in the future partnership when it manifests in physical form.

Joyce: Thank you. That sounds perfect and I am in complete agreement. I don't know when the time will come, but knowing that his Ba and mine are in touch and making all things fall in place, I have confidence that it will happen as it should.

While we are talking about the body and healing, I often see bursts of light in my visual field. I heard that they were called blue pearls in Hindu literature. They are mostly bright electric blue and appear for a moment and then disappear. Sometimes they can also be other colors. Would you comment on them?

Enlightened One: When my intentions are turned to the healing of your body, there is a slight temperature change in the magnetic field around your body and thus there is a discharge much like tiny lightening strikes

64

from one layer to another. There is much to know about what is happening in the healing process of anyone just by looking at the colors in the aura which can be photographed by aura cameras, so let us give you a bit of information about it.

Joyce: Great! I have a recent aura photo of myself. I want to know what it means.

Enlightened One: When the main color in an aura is red, it is an indication that the basic life force is being adjusted, possibly from dark red to lighter, brighter red. Think of the color red as corresponding to blood, which needs to be oxygenated and to flow freely, nourishing every cell in the body. Thus to see red in the aura is a generally wonderful indicator that the basic life energy is improving.

When the color lavender or violet appears, it is an indication that the nutrients of the body are being processed at a improving rate, thus it is an indicator of better digestion. As digestion is the basis of so much other improvement, it is a good sign indeed.

When the color yellow or orange appears, there are many lymph glands that are being repaired. Since the hormonal system needs to be in good repair for the body to function well, it is also a good sign.

When there is a lot of white light, it is a sign that the crown chakra has been opened and is receiving messages from Higher Mind. The powerful crown chakra acts like a shower and overflows into the rest of the aura. To have a large area of white all over the photo indicates that the channeling is strong enough to bless and heal the whole person. It is the sign of a healer's aura.

The color green is an indicator of something missing or misshapen in the aura. As we have discussed before, some people have a ding or dent in their aura due to longstanding emotional trauma. Green in your aura should be considered an indicator that some healing work on the emotional level is needed. Indeed a reader of auras can read the events of the life that have caused the malformation and receive a suggestion from the person's Enlightened One as to how to perform the healing. In lieu of any other information, simply doing a figure eight in the aura in front of the person is a good beginning.

Bright blue to dark blue are also a channeling indicator. When one dives deep into the blue dimension often, one almost always wears deep blue in one's aura. Those who visit on an occasional basis, use the light blue. If the blue is so dark that it turns to purple, the person is drawing from many lifetimes of access to the blue dimension.

Occasionally, one sees a mantle of gold around the outside of an aura, which indicates that one has therapeutic qualities of "presence." This means that others can gain the abilities of the one with the gold aura while in their presence. Thus one who is a healer gives healing while working with that energy and one who is a channeler gives channeling while working with that energy. There are a few other features that rarely show up and anyone who inquires will be given the needed information.

Joyce: Thank you. I looked closely at the aura photo of myself and I was following along with your descriptions, which seemed to fit what I know about myself very well. However, let me ask a few more questions.

I have seen some photos that show a person's aura nicely rounded with consistent colors and then others that seem to have spikes of color. What do the spikes indicate?

Enlightened One: When one has a spike of one color within another, that is an indicator that one energy is starting to operate in one area of the body, but not yet overall. A consistent field of color indicates that the healing or use of the ability is nearly complete and well balanced in the body.

Joyce: If one has had all of the colors in a consistent manner over a period of time what would that indicate?

Enlightened One: When one takes periodic photos and compares them over time, one could see a pattern of moving from red to lavender and then to yellow. It would indicate that the healing process is complete and they are coming into a state of wholeness and health. A very sick person should not be photographed, as the colors will be so pale as to not show at all. Nevertheless, even the pale colors will show a rotating cycle of the colors of the aura indicating an increase in the health of the body.

Joyce: That is very reassuring to know.

Enlightened One: Know that I bring much that is good to you each day. As your Ba, I am your own personal healer. When you join me with the Ba of the Christ Consciousness, the healing advances rapidly and more easily. That is the function of inviting in the Christ Consciousness Ba during the rejuvenation process. We will give more information about this in the next book.

Joyce: Just so Dear Readers everywhere can be sure of what we have just accomplished, let me go down my checklist. Correct me if I am wrong on any point.

Everyone can have a Ba, which is created by one's Peaceful One. It is often initiated when they simply make the wish to be happy or wish to know something or to do a good deed. Being on a spiritual path and opening to channel makes it possible to use them consciously. A Ba can only be used for the Highest Good, nothing else.

A Ba can operate in both dimensions and are mostly invisible, unless seen as orbs. They are made of light and are personal conscious entities of great strength and ability.

It is necessary to address one's Ba with a respectful and loving approach in order to establish conscious cooperation. It is the give and take of love and friendship that makes the relationship work. Requests for the Ba to perform the Highest Good can be made, and results manifested. They need to be followed by appreciation and gratitude. Appreciation recharges the relationship for the better and allows one to work with one's Ba better.

Once a request is made, the Conscious Mind should let the Ba take over and not interfere. However, a discussion about the progress of the work is possible and advisable because it generates more appreciation.

How'd I do? Are there any changes that you would like to make?

Enlightened One: None, my dear. You are a grace to work with and many more beings are getting in line to cooperate with you. Best let the highest and best of them take over the topic from here.

Joyce: Thank you. That felt so good. Just like best friends working together to help each other, only with a lot more power. I am getting the hang of how this cooperation with the spirit realm goes and am wondering who else is going to come forward to work with me. It should be interesting and I already know that only good will result.

Dear Reader, if you are following this, do not be afraid to try it yourself, for you have been using these types of resources all of your life, but perhaps never in a conscious way. So pause at this point and ask for something that you are sure is for the Highest Good and address your Ba as Enlightened One to see what happens. Once we get this relationship right, then there are more to come. Wonder what that is? Read on.

Chapter Five:
Christ Opens the Door to Other Dimensions

Peaceful One: We are about to further explore something that few can take seriously in this day and age, and that is the idea of alternate dimensions. In order to get a good footing on this topic, we would like to set the stage with another story of the Christ Consciousness as it proceeded to build a nation of peace in Ancient Egypt.

It was a sunny day on which the Great Pyramid was finally commissioned. It took 1,000 years to plan and build a society capable of sustaining the plan, and then another 100 years to build. On that sunny day long ago, there was a great clap of thunder and a major earth tremor. The geomagnetic energy gathered and concentrated by the pyramid was released and the surrounding land and sky responded to rebalance themselves. It was not that the foundation of the pyramid had not been properly laid, nor that the awareness of how to construct such a structure was at fault. Rather the design of the pyramid was so perfect that it called forth cooperation in the etheric dimension.

Indeed, the same man who had founded Egypt had reincarnated again to be present on that very special day. At his request, The Guardians of the Earth joined together to create an even greater opening to other dimensions so that the people could access all the gifts that existence in multiple dimensions could yield. Indeed the energy was so high and intentions were so good in both dimensions that joy expanded across the two dimensions. The thunder, booming across the plateau, although there were no clouds, reflected that it was a special moment in the history of mankind on the Earth.

Many of the spiritual relationships that had held the people in good stead for millennia during the development of Egypt needed to be celebrated and expanded. And so the gathering crowd of well-wishers could feel and hear the strength of the accord between the two dimensions. The Thirteen Guardians of the Earth, who had come in peace to form the Earth in the first place, had lain in rest for billions of years. On that day, however, they responded with great joy. This day of great thunder was the first test of faith for the gathered humans that they were indeed in the presence of a preternatural force of great magnitude.

If you had been in a distant town, say several hundred miles away, you would have felt the Earth shake and heard the thunder boom. In response to the kindness to be in touch once again, the Earth Guardians regarded this event as one in which to give great gifts. Thus instead of the usual speeches, ceremonial parades and such, there were peels of thunder, ground tremors, and much more signaling the presence of great etheric beings gathered to be of help. Indeed the etheric plane had never before been opened with such a prospect for benign outcomes. And for such a thing to happen was cause for much jubilant celebration on both sides of the dimensional barrier.

Remember that when souls incarnate on the Earth, each soul agrees to live in the Conscious Mind, which can be unaware of its original residence in the other dimension of spirit. Once the portal of transference between the two dimensions had been opened, however, there were humans who could not only remember their origin, but also to be consciously resident in two dimensions at once. This was a great leap forward in human evolution, and humans would never again be able to live in total grief with no relief available. Thus the love flowed in great abundance between the two dimensions. The gift of free speech between the etheric ones from the Blue Dimension of spirit existence and humans from the Physical Dimension was the cause of much appreciation on both sides.

With this, there was yet another thing that happened that day to consider. If you had been in a jet airplane and looked down upon the Giza Plateau, you would have seen a snake-like separation in the sand, bearing South East to North West. This was the result of the closing of a great gap that had opened on the day that the great continent of Atlantis sank. When this tectonic closing occurred, it opened a rift in the magnetic field of the ionosphere that, in turn, induced the counterpoint ley line to open under the Great Pyramid.

It was from this vast source of geo energy flowing through the ley line and the electromagnetic field around the Earth that the Pyramid drew the power to form a giant orb of light that soon floated above it. This giant orb provided a field of peacefulness within which the people lived. Indeed the orb is still blessing the Earth and will for all time. With the opportunity to rediscover its gift and to replicate it over and over again in other places, much needed Earth healing is due to occur.

Thus, those whose ancestors had survived the supposed natural disaster in Atlantis were frightened to think that such a disaster would happen at Giza as well. But such was not to be the case. In fact, those who had control of such forces were the tiny little orbs of the weather forces, namely the kindly Aurora, in contact with both the sky and the Earth. They moved so that nothing disastrous happened. Although some of the huge stones within the pyramid cracked, they will never fail and the energy for the doing of good that was set in motion on that day has lasted even unto today.

If you have not yet been introduced to the friendly Aurora, refer to *Book of the Highest Good,* Volumes 3 and 4. But let it be said that their advice is good advice. For their continued cooperation is what has kept the Earth in benign conditions for millennia. If you think that it is about time that you show some appreciation for these tiny little energy forces that control so much of your lives, you are correct.

Indeed it would also be in order to point out that there are none among you who can properly count the times that there have been benign conditions for the growing of your food, the raising of your children, and the taking of your journeys on your way in life. So it is with great appreciation that we give thanks with the words: *Auora Boreolis, we love you and acknowledge that you love us as well.* Thus, it is in gratitude to the Aurora for their faithful service in keeping the Earth pure, clean, and properly in orbit that we have begun this dialogue.

Joyce: So you are saying that the energy of joy in both dimensions affected the continental plates. Then the energy streams in the ionosphere cooperated to create the ley line under the Great Pyramid. When all were in place and balanced, an orb of high consciousness came to rest above the pyramid, giving accelerated contact with the etheric dimension. All of this was done under the guidance of the original founder of Egypt. That founder was a prior incarnation of Edgar Cayce and the commissioner of the Great Pyramid was the person of the Christ Consciousness.

Wow, is all that I can say. I had no idea and I certainly don't understand how all of this can be done. I take it that the ancient Egyptians didn't know either. They were following instructions from the Star Beings for over a thousand years to make all of this happen. The Star Beings must have laid a grand plan and meticulously used human cooperation to implement it. Wow! I have so many more questions to ask about this.

But as I think about it, I feel so much appreciation and love. To think that we could refurbish and replicate this same plan to enhance the Earth is a stunning thought. I suppose that it can all be done the same way, through mental communication with the Star Beings, which we have been doing all along in these books. Of course, Christ Consciousness is in charge of the whole plan.

I have to take a rest on that thought. This is a big thought. I need some fresh fruit and walk around the yard, something familiar. Wow.

+*+

Dear Reader, are you still here with me? You are in physical form reading words on the page just as I am in physical form writing it, but apparently we have company. We have our Peaceful Ones and the Star Beings. On top of that, our spirit Ba's are also present together and in cooperation, doing nothing but good. Remember when the Enlightened One was speaking to us and we discovered the existence of our Ba and all that it can do for good? In order to get to that point of view, we had to let go of our concepts of separation from our Creator and each other.

Did you notice how patiently Peaceful One explained it to us over and over again? When we finally gave up the idea that we could ever be separated, Peaceful One gave us the gift of a conscious connection with our Ba. How great is that?

I hope that you have been practicing that relationship and achieving great companionship with such a powerful being. But as is always the case, the Peaceful One takes us up in altitude once more to show who else is available for our relationships. Do you feel the excitement? Is the back of your neck feeling tingly? It is someone very special, another Wonderful One in that Cave of Consciousness we learned about. So let's proceed with love in our hearts and the grand knowing that we are Beloved Ones in the presence of our companion Beloved Ones.

Once again, we find that the inner world of mental contact with spirit beings is a fascinating one of truth and kindness and have come to crave it, have we not? It is such a truly great relationship that we are not willing to give it up because it has never done us any harm, and always gives much good. In this book, we have found that there are many more beings wishing to speak with us than we could ever imagine. We will gradually learn their particular functions or gifts and how to access them whenever we need more peace. Each has a particular gift to give from their level of existence and it is all part of a plan. Our part is to experience and appreciate their gift in our existence, now so enriched by their companionship.

But I am only running on with my happiness to be here with you reading these conversations. Let's ask the Peaceful One to begin again and to give us once again the gift of peace and companionship.

+*+

Peaceful One: How happy is happy if it is not joyous for one and all? Thus we send our regards to all seekers that they may all have many a happy journey of peace in these new discussions dealing with the residents of a great community of spirit beings. As always, we must prepare the minds of the readers for taking the path that they desire, so we pose this suggestion.

If one lives in a decent-sized home, but wanted a bigger one, then one might consider remodeling with the option of expanding beyond the current borders of one's home. This is exactly what we intend to do with the Dear Readers who ventured into the present timeline for the doing of good for the Earth and its people. Some may assume that it is already too late or that there are conditions that are too great to be remedied for the Earth to be in peace. This is not the case, but in order to realize the magnitude of the contribution made by members of the etheric side, one must be introduced to some of their other accomplishments.

Therefore, we would like to take the topic of home remodeling to the location of the planets Mars and Venus and find out how the three inner planets, Earth, Mars, and Venus came to be known as the three Sisters of Life. As such, they have helped each other over and over again to regain atmosphere and to protect life-giving environments only to fall into disuse again and again. Most importantly, let it be known that not all three were ever in retreat all at the same time. For each has seeded the other with life over and over again.

Seated upon a bench in a crime-ridden neighborhood, one might think of one's neighbor as being not particularly friendly, but that is not the case with the planets in the solar system under the care of the Christ Consciousness. These three sisters have been in love with life since the beginning of creation, and are ruled by a kind and benevolent entity, ably assisted by the tiny orbs of weather-creating beings.

Much like these much smaller beings called orbs which exist even within the human body, a planet is a unit composed of orbs having the qualities of much energy in the form of mass, gravity, spin, and direction of travel. As a planet spins and travels through space, it is amply cared for by many orb beings. For space is not empty. It is populated by spirit forms searching for a way to be of service. Thus as one planet decides to rest for a while, the space orbs attend to its needs by bringing many minerals and elements floating in space for their use. They also remove what is in oversupply, thus creating a balance.

The orbs of space also serve the Earth, inhabited by living physical creatures such as plants, animals, and humans. They remove what is to be recycled elsewhere and bring in other resources that are needed. There is a great relationship between and among the orbs and the planets. If one would only open one's mind to them, the whole community of orbs would empty their hearts and minds of so much good as to once more make the pyramids shake, for such was the good that was done on the opening day of the Great Pyramid.

For as long as the pyramids have been standing, they have been serving the purpose of facilitating such transactions between the Earth and the space community in a conscious way. Thus there were many at that time that could speak to space orbs and the planet orbs, etc. In finding that none were right or wrong, but all living their own cycles of life, ably assisted by their companions, the people felt that everything was right in the universe and thus it was. In finding that the Creator of all of this must be responsible, there were many who made the effort to learn to be in communication with the Creator of the solar system in particular.

Although the Christ Consciousness was named the great Ra in those days of the Egyptians, today it would be better understood to say God the Creator and the Son who cares for this solar system, in concert with the communicator orb beings. These entities are, in short, the three companions of Creation, often referred to as the Trinity.

For the purpose of this book, we'd like to present yet another way to be in dialogue with these originators and caretakers of physical reality in this solar system. Let's call them the Triune Makers of Peace. Having named them correctly and found them to be the good friends who gave life a place to live and play that is benign and peaceful, we can now enter into a relationship with them. Thus let us begin with a question.

Joyce, would you start the conversation? We will initiate the connections and your Ba will translate into your vibration and language so you can transcribe it for Dear Readers everywhere.

Joyce: OK. I feel like this is a momentous event for me and for the Earth. I understand that I am talking to the ones who created life on this planet as well as the whole solar system. They maintained it and established communication within and outside this solar system. Am I correct about that? I am humbled and ever so grateful that you did such a benign and beautiful thing.

Triune Makers of Peace: We three know that you might wonder about such an event, but we created only what millions and billions of small and large beings wanted to partake of. Let us start off with a little prayer for all who wish to be in communication with us:

Lord, our Father and Creator of our physical universe, who made a Son to be the compassionate caretaker of it and all beings within it and the Bringer of great communication, let us be at peace. For peace was your original intention and having found it to be productive of great grace and beauty, we avow of ourselves to be nothing else. And in knowing and desiring that, we are eligible to participate with all of the other beings desiring the same thing. Thus we are no longer outsiders, but rather the beloved members of a great family of grace givers and receivers. We give our consent for peace to go on forever. Amen.

And now, with much grace at your request, what would you like to ask us?

Joyce (deep breath): I am so awed! I have to think for a minute. OK, here's a good question: Why did you create the physical universe? It seems that the spirit dimension is a great place, but the physical universe is so different that even fear can exist.

Triune Makers of Peace: Our peace is your peace. If you choose to roam far and wide, there is no danger, pain, or suffering to be had anywhere. Whence have you come to the conclusion that fear and its offspring, pain and suffering, have any existence?

Joyce: Because I have experienced it.

Triune Makers of Peace: What one would experience as pain and suffering is caused by the choice to retain a picture of reality that is too small and mean to be of much use. Therefore, follow us along with a new line of thought and find what was put into place for peace to be resident everywhere and at all times, no exceptions. Fear is an illusion easily overcome. However, since it is an option for the Conscious Mind to entertain fear, we offer some insights about it.

The design of the physical dimension was to provide a place to develop a unique decision-making mechanism: The freedom to love or not to love. You know it as free will. With that in mind, it was necessary to have no memory of the nature of the Higher Mind. For even a small memory of the great love and support available in the spirit dimension would preclude all decision not to love. Without this memory of love, it was indeed possible to know fear and to live under its shadow. Thus you need the will to *decide* not to fear. With this, you will be able to recover the memory and full knowledge of the great love of the Creator. In other words, those with free will must choose to love over and over again until he or she is able and willing to be love itself, a most satisfying state of being.

Without full memory of love, the experiences of physical human life need to be reinterpreted as grace, even though they feel like grief. Thus life begins a long series of choices to love or not to love through which people come to be convinced of the love they are living within. With this, the existence of the Higher Mind

81

opens. For how could one, who is separate from the largest and most beautiful part of oneself, ever be happy? Indeed the Conscious Mind is only a small part of the Higher Mind, but they are the same being. The true story of physical existence is one of reuniting one part of oneself to the other. What a great love story that makes, don't you think?

Joyce: I know what you are talking about. I remember so many times when I felt alone and in misery, only to turn to the Peaceful One and find all kinds of help and comfort. I eventually got to the point that I abhorred residing only in the Conscious Mind. I yearned for Higher Mind. Then the Peaceful One healed my Conscious Mind so that it became as beautiful as the Higher Mind. These days, my Conscious Mind lives in mostly peaceful cooperation with Higher Mind.

Triune Makers of Peace: Who then is responsible for the outcome of your experiences, you or me?

Joyce: We together. We cooperated and found our way back together again and we live in peace. That is how I am communicating with you today.

Triune Makers of Peace: Well, then, let's make light of the why or the how, and just rejoice that it has happened. For once again, a great burst of joy has taken place, much like the first opening of the Great Pyramid. Did you hear any thunder or feel the ground shake?

Joyce: Actually, yes. Not long ago, there was a strong thunderstorm that went through my area and I wondered if the Auroras were sending me confirmation that something big was happening. I often feel the Earth shift a tiny little bit. I hope that I am not causing it.

Triune Makers of Peace: All of us are in accord and there is a need for the shifting of resources so that all can be in harmonious vibrations. The function of weather and earth shifts is to rebalance energy. It is all completely normal and happens thousands of times a day all over the planet. The Earth is a quite vibrant and responsive place. Its companion planets are the same.

Joyce: Yes, tell me more about Mars, Earth, and Venus – the Sisters of Life. Did Mars and Venus have the same type of life that we are familiar with on Earth? I know that the conditions are quite different on each.

Triune Makers of Peace: When conditions for life are present, there are many who apply… so, no and yes. There have been many strange life forms on all three planets from time to time and many more to come, but mostly humans have been an Earth life experience.

Joyce: So do some life forms still exist on Mars and Venus and why does Venus rotate the other direction from the others?

Triune Makers of Peace: Yes, there are certain types of life on Mars that would defy description on Earth. The atmosphere is not conducive to much that is Earthlike, but in due time there will be more atmosphere as the kindly orbs of Aurora decide to form a new and more benign atmosphere.

Venus is yet to decide on her fate. For the time being, it erupts with lava and has a highly sulfurous environment in which only sulfur-tolerant life forms can live. However after a great deal of time, her atmosphere will again create much that was there in times past. As for her rotation, there is none who have seen it any other way. Being in reverse orbit, it is a place of much reversal mentality where one can, in spirit form, work out much that is amiss to peace. Many of those who sojourn there in spirit between lifetimes come back to Earth in a much more loving form. That is why it has a reputation of being the planet of love.

Joyce: I think that you are saying that Venus is a place of removal of barriers to love. When souls spend time there between lifetimes, they come into their next lifetime much better prepared to love. It is a place of grief relief. The counterclockwise spiral performs grief relief and Venus rotates that same direction.

Thanks for the information about the three sisters of life. It makes me think of the whole solar system as being an interconnected and cooperative community. I don't know why we would ever think otherwise. Everything else in creation is complex and interconnected.

You talked about Christ Consciousness coming at the time of the opening of the Great Pyramid. Was that in physical form or in spirit form and what exactly did he do?

Triune Makers of Peace: Should one of us remain in physical form and the others in spirit, we would all cooperate just as well, as you pointed out. Thus it would be wise to say that he was in both forms and that he opened the great door of the pyramid consciousness by testing his own strength. As the architect, Hermes, he entered into the King's chamber when the pyramid was finished. The room was bare except for the granite container. He lay in the granite container to change his consciousness from human to Higher Mind, much like you do today when you meditate.

In doing so, he had put himself into a perfect vibrating machine. When he entered into our dimensions with joyful strength, the rock walls began to vibrate and a few cracks began to show. No harm was done and soon he was in his spirit form and on his way to his fatherly home, so to speak. Upon arriving, he inquired of the Star Beings and requested that they be in preparation for more inter-dimensional communication. He was greeted with much accord in the spirit dimension. The united presence of the star beings was made known to the populace in physical dimension as thunder and lightening in the cloudless sky. The startled people did not know what to think. When Hermes emerged from the pyramid, he explained it all to them and many came and went into the chamber to experience the same thing for many thousands of years to come. At one point, Christ himself, in the form of Isaiah, closed the pyramid. Isaiah was the Jewish immigrant who knew himself to be blessed, but also knew that the world was not fit for the knowing of such transit opportunities at that time.

On Pentecost, Christ told his disciples that they would receive many gifts of knowing from the spirit of communication later called the Holy Spirit. In saying this for his apostles, Christ was asking once again to be admitted to the inter-dimensional conversation on behalf of mankind. As he was doing that, a wide doorway was opened for communication between the dimensions. He gave the disciples the password by saying: *My peace I give you*. As the disciples departed on Pentecost, they could translate many languages through mind transference with spirit beings and to find their way safely all over the Earth as they preached the Gospel. They worked miracles and made much good, all by communication through the dimensional portal.

Thus Pentecost was the second time that the dimensional door, created at the time that the Great Pyramid was opened and it has remained open since, waiting for one and all to proceed in conversation. Your current effort to portray how blessed an event it is to open to one's channel is just such a cooperative effort in support of His will. Congratulations for being of one mind with His. Indeed, His is a great mind and will do whatever is needed to portray your books in a kind way to anyone who comes looking for the portal to heavenly awareness or enlightenment.

Joyce: Wow! I had no idea. I do remember that Christ said that he was going to prepare a place in His Father's house for his disciples. That must be what he meant. Once again, it all comes back to the reuniting of the two minds with the help of the Great Oneness. That is essentially what Revered Healer did to get the information that he used to create the foundation of Egyptian peace. I know that opening to channel was what I did to be able to find my own personal peace and to be able to sit and do this type of work. Sweet! So sweet, and it's really very simple, but, oh so beautiful.

OK, so now there is free inter-dimensional spirit travel and communication between the dimensions. Our Ba translates the communication into the form of psychic readings so that we can participate. In order to use the portal, we have to be at peace. Then it brings only more peace. So cool! What's next?

Triune Makers of Peace: How much peace do you need to make peace over the whole Earth? With that question, we are not expecting you to give us the answer, but rather asking you to think a little bit about the enormity of the task. With billions of people – all beset with active Conscious Minds, all firmly attached to personal gain and verified by social structures – how far does one have to go to find the peace that surpasses that type of understanding? That is the question.

Joyce: I suppose quite a lot of peace. But I know that you have a plan. You have hinted at it before. Remember you told me to make the etheric pyramid at my farm and then the Christ Consciousness came and presided over it, giving peace 24/7? Surely that is something like what your plan is like. But what else is in the plan?

Triune Makers of Peace: How come, as you are wont to say, does it take so long for just one author to make herself known to the general public and not be ridiculed for being unrealistic? How long will it take until not a single child is left hungry or abused? How long until a marriage contract is taken so seriously that never is there a divorce for lack of trying? How long until all people are accepted and equally entitled to the goods and services of the world economy? How long until the twist of time comes unraveled?

Joyce: I got all of that until you said the twist of time becomes unraveled. What does that mean?

Triune Makers of Peace: When one has a need to be at peace, one has little respect for time. Thus, those living in peace neither progress nor regress in age. They essentially remain intact until they turn their minds to the transference of their life energy to another dimension. What would it be like when a community of these peaceful ones generates ageless people on a consistent basis? Is that when the agents of grief start looking elsewhere besides their own doubt and fear? For human society, time is considered the most immutable and fearful part of life. The current thinking is that all must know and accept that they will grow old and apparently perish. How will their world tremble when it is shown that such is not the case?

Joyce: Well, I hadn't thought of ageless people. I guess ageless people living in peace would be very astounding to the world and, with the Internet, the word would travel the globe very quickly. So if that is necessary to increase respect for peace, how do we do that? I know that I am growing older, but to grow old and die does not bother me as much as it used to because I know my spiritual side so well. I know that my transition would be easy and very rewarding.

Triune Makers of Peace: With that done, there is no time like the present to address the coming attraction announced so long in the past as to be forgotten. *For you are all gods*, the prophet announced. Before you catch your breath on that statement, let us tell you a little story about a baby born with no lungs with which to breathe. What was the status of that infant? With no lungs to use for breathing, how could it live? With no living infant, how could the mother and father be consoled. One moment, there were no lungs and then suddenly, there were two healthy lungs ready for the first breath of air.

Joyce: Who are you talking about? Did this really happen?

Triune Makers of Peace: No one that you know could have done this miracle, but Christ Himself. And so you wonder for a minute of what use is a connection with Christ Consciousness and we are telling you that the miracle of the lungs and many more will be performed in His name just for the asking. Then people will know who and what is at work on the peaceful Earth and many doubts will cease.

Joyce: So complete access to Christ Consciousness gives me the privilege of asking for these kinds of miracles? Wow and wow! Surely there has to be something more required. I have prayed for many people in their time of need and no miracles that I am aware of have happened. Tell me more.

Triune Makers of Peace: How would you like to know that your friend who passed away knew that he had so much more to offer than he could do in physical form and had a great desire to do it. Thus we have granted him status as one of the askers of miracles for the physical dimension. In the Great Oneness there is no one who is denied this privilege. Within human society it would indeed take a great commitment to achieve. Just ask your Magician/Healer friend to take care of healing problems and we will answer for him and support his every effort.

Joyce: Oh what a fine journey he decided to take. Magician/Healer would you speak to me about this?

Magician/Healer: What would you like me to say? I've been talking with the great healers and asking all kinds of questions and none have come forth with anything more grand than what you have just ascertained about the Triune Makers of Peace. How could anyone in spirit form deny their power and place to do such miracles? After all, it was they who created the physical universe to be so benign and even set the time and the place for all of this to happen. So without feeling the least bit unrealistic or silly, I'd say that the human race could say goodbye to aches and pains unless such aches and pains are specifically chosen by a Conscious Mind to experience. Then humans can say hello to great peace so that all that is wholesome and grand will follow.

Joyce: Well you can start with me. I hereby officially deny access to any pain and suffering in my body or experience. I officially ask for the miracles of bodily preservation that are required to convince people that peace is a viable force in the universe worth investing in. OK, so there, I've done it.

So what exactly have I done?

Magician/Healer: Well what did you intend to do? That is exactly what you have done. I have only assisted in taking the request as far as it can go until it reaches the doors of heaven so to speak. Now it is time to stop with the doubt and to address making ready for a different kind of dialogue. Why don't you ask Triune Makers of Peace what they have in mind next?

Joyce: Thank you and I know that it is you sending this message because of your directness of speech and humor. You are still a good friend to us all. Yes, Triune Makers of Peace, what do you have in mind now?

Triune Makers of Peace: We being three have no need to be separate, so we need to be present in a new way to show you a different view of reality. What you are about to hear is yet another dream sequence that you had, of which we are responsible. It will portray why and how you were made to be the way that you are. May we proceed in a new part of this book?

Joyce: Once again, I am propelled into a new experience. I have met the Trinity and listened to how the doors between dimensions were opened and then told to use my connection with the Magician/Healer to request miracles. Miracles, that is, from the perception of the Conscious Mind, but ordinary normal reality to the Higher Mind. If I can accept that, then I can accept much more. Let's go for it.

Chapter Six:
Christ Consciousness Needs No Return

Dear Reader, would you like to read my personal manifesto? Here it is:

No matter where I go or what I do, there you are, Peaceful One, leading me into more and more good. And that is the way that all of my lifetimes have been and that is all that the future will bring. I am in a time, place, and condition to be benignly loved and cared for. I have no fear, for fear is the harbinger of much grief and I have no desire for it. I am at rest and in total security, being in contact with the next dimension where much good awaits anyone who asks. As such, I wish to serve the needs of all beings to be in peace.

Getting myself to this point has been a very long process of about six years and I know that it is not all complete yet. But I am far enough along to see that it is true for me and can be for anyone. How did I get here? Well, it is a very long story, but I will summarize it for the moment of consideration that it deserves.

At the worst point of my life – when I was abandoned by a spouse, out of work, and living alone in an isolated place – I elected to turn inward for help. I sat by a sunny window by myself for many, many hours, days, and months listening to my own thoughts. Noticing the difference between the fearful thoughts of the Conscious Mind and the peaceful and benign thoughts of the Higher Mind, I made another fateful decision. I decided to honor the Higher Mind and to subordinate the Conscious Mind to the leadership of the Higher.

Things began to get a bit better and I was encouraged, but it was very slow. That's when the real work began. I had to face the fears, which grew like crabgrass wherever I stepped, even in the good times. With that task ahead, I knew that I was in for a struggle that would appear to be very unrewarding and laborious at first and only later reap significant results. In short, it was an uphill struggle that seemed to be going nowhere. But I had developed a process that worked pretty well. I will describe it for you in case you might want to use it as well.

When I would feel sad, angry, or unhappy, I would ask myself the question: *What am I afraid of?* I did this because I came to understand that it is fear and only fear that makes us unhappy. The answers that I got ranged from the fear of being left alone and unsupported, to the fear of being abandoned and separated from those who loved me. Each time that the fears arose and made me sad, I would look the ugly fear in the eye and ask for the antidote thought.

The antidote thought could be a simple one: *Only one or two people rejected you. All others accept you.* Another antidote thought was: *My early experiences with relationships were very discouraging, but that was a long time ago. These days, I have more options and there are many people interested in knowing and caring about me.* Whatever the antidote thought was, I had to use it over and over again because the same fear would arise over and over again. It was indeed like pulling weeds. They just grew back. But if I was persistent enough, they grew weaker and I could control them easier and better.

Finally, as I had fewer crash-and-burn episodes of depression, I stabilized in my outlook about my future. One day I looked at things and decided that my life was going pretty well. At that moment, I approved of myself and I turned an important corner of grief relief. When I eventually named myself as a Fortunate One, then more and better things happened. That reinforced my conviction that my fate was a good one. I could compare the recent good developments against the past painful experiences caused by fear. The difference was so obvious and clear that there was no contest as to which direction was the one for me. Thus I resolved to never go back to accepting any fear. As Martin Luther King said, *"I decided to stick with love. Hate is too great a burden to bear."* I could see that to give in to any fear or anger would only doom me to be unhappy and ultimately sick and old. I was done with it so completely that I would never turn back.

In order to give me an easy and effective method of resisting fears, the Peaceful One gave me a meditation technique that worked very well and I will share it with you now. Get very relaxed in a comfortable position and begin deep breathing. Listen to your breath going in and out realizing that the bringing in of air is giving you life and the expelling of air is removing toxins that are harmful. As your mind brings up thoughts, apply this one simple rule. If you like the thought or image, say to yourself *Thank You*. If you don't like the thought or image, say to yourself, *I give my peace to that*. Then go back to listening to your life-giving breathing. When thoughts come again, give the same responses and go back to breathing. Repeat this over and over again. Just do it a few minutes a day, anytime when you are reflecting on your life. The net result is that your dialogue with your Peaceful One is enhanced and you are far less fearful.

That is how I got to this place of security and peace, but I suspect that in asking to be of service to all beings, that there is much more to the story. So that is how I have come to the title of this section: *Christ Consciousness Has No Need to Return*. Do I know what it means exactly? No, I don't, but I know who to ask and who to trust. So here goes, are you with me? If you are still struggling with fears, hang in there but read on with curiosity to see where it leads us.

+*+

Joyce: Peaceful One, please explain the phrase: Christ Consciousness has no need to return.

Peaceful One: When Christ left Earth in his transfigured form, he made a promise to be with his followers wherever they went. His promise to return was essentially fulfilled at that point. His etheric being was being replicated many times over as etheric doubles or Ba to serve as companions to walk with each of his disciples. The apostles understood it that way because they could feel His presence and understand His thoughts. And so as they traveled and gave the good word of the Gospels, each had the use of His Ba to perform miracles and to consult with as to the best use of their time, talents, and energies. When they passed on the good word of His message of the Highest Good, many believers asked for the same gift and were given their own version of the Ba of Christ. Thus there are many replicas of the etheric Christ walking around the planet in search of someone to heal, to comfort, and to help. It is with honesty and truth that we state that Christ has no need to return. He never left.

With that being said, there are many more who have engaged in past life experiences with Him who carry a Ba of Him in a slightly different nature: His Native American form, Egyptian form, Tibetan form, and so many more. Earth is populated with many lovers of the Christ Consciousness and they all know and love each other. If one, such as you, comes along to do some good and tells one and all to contact their Ba in a conscious manner, there is all the more good to be had. One who is in conscious communication with Him can share His words and inform their lives with His guidance and wisdom. As He did all of His life, Christ first heals and then teaches. Thus in finding that no Ba goes asleep, even while the physical bodies are sleeping, the Ba are indeed awake and active in doing good not only in the bodies of the followers, but also with their families and communities. No one is alone and no one is without His help. We would like to give a prayer for anyone to use to establish conscious contact with the Christ

Consciousness and to request his presence in that etheric form.

Prayer for the Presence of the Christ Consciousness

God has blessed us with the presence of his only Son whom we know as the Christ Consciousness and we rejoice in knowing and loving Him. His peace is enormous and far stronger than our own and we seek to live within it. Therefore, speaking with the right of children of the ever-living God who created all physical reality, we request and agree to live in peace with the presence of the Christ Consciousness. Please allow us to be sure of His presence with a sign that we will know as coming from Him. And so it is with gratitude that we sing the song of peace giving and allow it to dominate our lives and hearts. We wish conscious contact with His loving heart and wise mind. And thus it is. Amen.

Peaceful One: With this one prayer said over and over again in the company of peace lovers, the Earth will be transformed, not by technology (although much good technology will be given and effectively used), but by the heart and mind of the original Giver of Peace upon the three planets and the solar system. With that we are at peace and need nothing else to say. Let peace reign in all forms, ways and circumstances for it has no hiding place and does not need any permission to succeed.

Joyce: This is a stunning moment in my life. I have said the prayer with heartfelt intention and feel the gentle presence of One so profoundly loving that I cannot begin to say what He can do for me and for us all. Amen is indeed the only word.

Let us hear from Him what He has to say at this time.

Christ Consciousness: All of those who live in me, and I in them, have been tested with their own fears. In resisting those fears, they want companionship with my great heart. Thus let us continue with more readings to help and assist this precious place of life with the heartfelt intention to bring peace to lovers of peace everywhere.

Joyce: What you have just given us is a very precious gift. It means that we can cohabit with you and join you in bringing peace to the Earth. This is something that I'd never want to live without. Please tell me more about how to maintain this precious gift and use it wisely.

Christ Consciousness: Would you want me to live anywhere but in the best of homes? Make your heart and your home peaceful for I love peace. Would you want to be companions with me on the best of terms? Set up a lively conversation between us every day and ask for the many things that you need each day to live in peace. And when I give it, thank me, for that is all that I want. Being surrounded with the children of God in perfect union and joy is about the best that life can get for me. I am a family man, after all, and I visit my family all over the world.

Should but one of the Gentle Readers say the prayer and honestly ask for the Christ Consciousness energy form to live within his or her heart, it would transform his or her part of the world into a fine home for me to expand on my gracious healing and peace. To do so allows me to do the same for many more. This is by far the best gift that anyone could give me. These are the ones who are disturbed by media portrayals of the abused ones, unable to maintain life in economic poverty, disease, and crime. They will use my Presence to ask for all people to be healed, helped, and added to the respected community at large. I hear all that you say, think, and feel and I will be there to help with all of the good that you wish to manifest.

I love our life together as a human population and even more now that I have been invited into the hearts and minds of society in such an easy and obviously conscious way. With that, I bid you adieu for now. Go rest and be assured that your particular plight is no less important to me than the plight of any others. I love to see you happy and in the arms of another so blessed as to be with you, both in great appreciation of the other.

Chapter Seven:
Peace Heals

Peaceful One: If one has a penchant for fear, then there is much fear to be had. If one has a penchant for love, then there is much love to be had. Therefore, let us proceed with yet another variation on the meditation technique that we gave earlier.

Once you are relaxed, do the slow and steady breathing until it can be sustained without any effort. There is a moment of subliminal suggestibility that hypnotists use to evoke the subconscious. This is the moment to suggest that instead of being fearful, that you wish to live in peace and love. As a simple symbol of your intention, imagine the infinity sign to stand before you. If you practice this regularly, you cannot be in error of your wishes. Thus we find that yet another great gift of existence is given on the Earth plane. We desire that everyone use it to live the life that they want.

Infinity sign

Joyce: This sounds easy and pleasant. I will try it and report back what I experienced.

Twenty minutes later....

Joyce: Well, I had no trouble reaching the point of easy breathing, but not yet falling asleep. I made a circle of my fingers, thumb to index finger in each hand and linked them together to make the infinity sign. To me it seemed that the left would be an exit for the fear and the right would be an entrance to the peace. So I firmly thought to myself: *Remove all fear. Place peace and love in my life.* Then I fell asleep.

When I woke, I asked Peaceful One if I had done the job right and I understood that yes, I did. Just to compare notes, I would like to ask Peaceful One what it feels like to be in the presence of Christ Consciousness.

Peaceful One: At first, the Christ Consciousness has a very unique healing effect by which the body, which Christ designed, is healed and perfected. For example if a person's legs were bowed, they would lengthen and straighten. If his eyesight was poor, it would rectify.

Then the attention would go to the heart and each cell would be treated to perfection, one at a time. The heart is the organ of life infusion, so the more perfectly the cells function, the more life energy is available.

Then there is the perfection of the sense of peace and security like that of a child who playfully goes from one activity to another without much thought or worry, aware that there is always a parent nearby to protect, guide, and provide what is needed. Such a child would receive nothing but loving words and intentions even if a correction were needed.

Finally, there is the urge to pursue the path of service that most interests and pleases the individual. With no fear for one's security and total confidence that one will be provided for, one just proceeds to do what one wants to do to help others. Then one lives in peace and happiness until one needs to pursue more on a higher plane of existence.

Joyce: This sounds pretty nice to me, so I think that I will always have the request that I live in the body of the etheric form or double of the Christ Consciousness. It will be interesting to see how that kind of companionship unfolds. But really, who cares what it would, precisely, look like? It would all be good and of the general nature of the peace plan for the Earth.

Peaceful One: When one releases grief and invites in peace in the form of the intentional cross of gold (gold is the color of giving service) or with the help of a crystalline form in the vicinity, it will be even more efficient. There is no other way for humans to be rejuvenated mentally, emotionally, and physically, all within the design and plan of the original founder of life on Earth.

With this said, there is no better way for Joyce to perform her service for humanity than to document how it feels to be subjected to the Ba of the Christ Consciousness for thirty days. Thus we propose a new book entitled *Diary of Rejuvenation* be started and see what we get in terms of a response not only from her and her body/mind, but all others who follow the same advice.

With that we recommend that all who are interested, set the same intention and participate in this great experiment of peace as it unfolds. You have nothing to lose but illness, grief, and suffering. We have torched the pyramid of grace and enlightened the sky of misunderstanding about what life on Earth is all about. This book is to be followed by yet another or two or three books. Where this conversation will end is not the question when so many apply with so many questions and needs.

It is not a publishing empire or a living that we seek, but rather the service of the whole human race to be in sync with the Christ Consciousness. For wherever He leads is a good place to be. Fulfillment of His service of healing is about to be accomplished in the lives of those who inquire.

Thus we leave this chapter as we began, in peace, and no harm was ever done nor will it ever be. For the guarantee of all of this is for one to be suited to the task of being happy and then to disperse the necessities for peace to all others. For peace is the force of the universe to expand, explore, recapture, and re-advertise the presence of He who lives here with all of the offspring of God. Let peace be in your lives and in your hearts, for it has a habit of propagating itself into the Presence of God.

Chapter Eight:
Through the Portal and Then What?

After re-reading the prior seven chapters, I am left with a question: *Where does one begin to give service?* I think that I know a little of what the apostles must have felt as they set out to carry the intention of Christ in their travels and teachings. Somehow I have to bring all of this down to the words that I need to say and deeds I need to do. I pondered the content of this book for several days and suddenly I got requests to teach and to help some people who had heard of my books. I jumped in and did what I could, using my contact with the Peaceful One and the Christ Consciousness. Here is the dialogue that followed the help that I gave.

+*+

Joyce: I have been enjoying giving readings and classes to many people who seem to come alive with purpose and joy when they hear the messages from The Peaceful One. I am so glad to see the effect. There must have been far more happening than what I said or did. Would you comment on how these readings, classes and sessions are supported on the etheric side?

Peaceful One: When one sets out to do good, there is a good intention at work, which attracts the attention of those in etheric form who wish to use their own brand of gift giving. Thus many people come to these readings and classes wanting something so grand that they dare not say it. They want to be truly loved by someone who can give them all that they need to be whole and happy. Is that not what has propelled you on for so many more pages than you ever thought that you would be writing?

Joyce: Very much so and you are right about other people wanting the same thing. I was talking to a woman who made the statement that she had never been loved (meaning by a partner). I remember at one point making that same statement myself. It doesn't mean that we have never had loving people in our lives that loved us in the best way that they could, but it does mean that we needed much more than a partner did, or could, give. We assumed that a partner would be able to give that intimate love, but that proved futile. We all have a great thirst for love that never seems to be able to be satisfied. We just want to be loved and loved and loved. Is that what you are talking about?

Peaceful One: How is one who loves, capable of only a little love? If love is to be given, it does so in a manner that constantly unfolds, expands, and delivers much more than is expected. Indeed everyone knows when they are loved and when they are not. To live in fear and grief is to live under the intention to do harm and to live in peace is to live under the influence of love. To make the happy decision to avoid fear is to love oneself into bliss consciousness.

Joyce: You mean that limited love is a contradiction in terms. Is it an all-or-nothing kind of thing?

Peaceful One: When one realizes that one consists of enough love to make a whole new universe, then one needs to be in the presence of that love at all times. Indeed one would avoid all intention for harm. So why not stop with the what-if condition of living in doubt and just go for the final true version of who you really are? In short, why not get rid of the doubt about you being a source for unconditional love for everyone who interacts with you? "What-if" love is sort of like playing a game of "Who Done It?" Did the butler do it? Did the houseguest do it? We can't know until we find the one who did it. Face the facts. You are love. You live on love and give love in all of its many varieties of forms. Everyone else is the same way, but they might not consciously know it.

When one finds love to be so involving and completely satisfying, but yet never ending and constantly evolving, then one has no option other than to admit that one is addicted to such love. One becomes what one loves and thus one gives as good as one gets. Everyone is fully capable of giving unlimited, unconditional love. And with such giving, one never seems to run out of joy. Does it not seem curious that people can doubt such a thing?

Joyce: Yes, that is essentially my question. How does this all work so beautifully, so benignly, so exponentially, and yet we can doubt it?

Peaceful One: When one wants to be loved beyond all prior experiences of love and release the doubt that results from disappointing experiences, one has to take the great leap of loving oneself from the depths of one's soul. And in being seen as good and lovable just because you did so, then you begin to love out of the pure joy of being lovable. Being loved by yourself, you bypass all manner of grief and pain in one giant leap. The greatest part of this gift of love for yourself is to resist fear, judgment, and limited thinking. All good comes from that gift. Once you see the results, you fall in love with being in love.

Thus there is the blessing of one to be in love with love itself, for love is indeed a mighty force of creation and never does one come to it without being gifted. Therefore we can safely say that love makes more love in countless benign and beautiful ways. Is that not so for you and all others who come to see you?

Joyce: Yes, that is what I find happening. So you are saying that love is a creative thing that expands and opens all new ways of being in love. You are also saying that it is the essential reason for the universe in the first place. I remember the quote from Genesis regarding God's work of creation: "And God said that it is good." In making something good, God gave love and it was the love given that made it beautiful, benign, and expanding.

Peaceful One: When one loves something in order to give good, then indeed one gives love. The reverse is to view something as unworthy of good so therefore giving harm is acceptable. Does that sound like the world of doubt of which you have been subscribing? In short, the question of you being good enough to be loved turns into the realization that giving good enough is being loved. Have no doubt that you are good and loveable and give good because of the love of doing so.

Joyce: I hope I never again have the pain of the doubt of being good enough. I will have to laugh and say to myself: "If I can give good enough, then I must be good." How can I give this blessing to those who come asking for peace?

Peaceful One: When one does a reading intending great blessings, those who come for the blessings also open to their innermost source of such blessings. Thus we offer this suggestion: When doing readings for people, occasionally allow them an interlude of music or meditation in which to connect themselves to the inner source with which you are channeling, namely me. When they realize that I am the One that they have been talking to all of their lives, the one who loved them and helped them, they will cozy up for more. And when they do, they will find that as great a love as I have to offer, there is yet another greater than I with even more love and on and on. Isn't this cave of consciousness fun?

Joyce: Indeed! You have also touched on a problem of doing this kind of work. I wish to share the blessings to all who come seeking help and I clearly state that they can do it themselves and experience the love that you give. Often it takes a little while for them to gain the confidence to make a strong connection. So I often do several sessions with people and even stay in contact for a longer time. This process has blessed me with many new friends. But I can see how so many people, needing so much, could overwhelm me. So I see that you are telling me that I only have to open the door. Once inside, people will find you and all of the Wonderful Ones.

Peaceful One: Yes this is the plan that was used since the beginning of the ancient Mystery Schools. The teachers only had to show people where to seek to find who's behind the blue door.

As you find more information about the hieroglyphs of ancient Egypt, you will come to understand the great statue figures carrying the ankh in their hand or laying their hands on their knees, were set there to form a union of energies between a giver and a listener. Then you will recognize that these are indeed the Great Ones who listened to Higher Mind long enough to be able to transfer the energetic openings to anyone who came looking for them.

Joyce: Well, I admit that I have always wondered why the ancient Egyptians made such huge statues of seated figures. The faces seem peaceful and benign and their hands are often on their knees. In wall murals, they are sometimes shown as walking or standing figures ready for a journey or a task, holding the ankh in one hand and leading the way for others. Tell me more about these figures.

Peaceful One: If you were about to show your fitness for doing a grand championship event of some kind, would you not announce to the world that you are indeed ready to go? Indeed, these figures were often travelers seeking to go on a long journey. They announced their intention to travel the Earth in search of others interested in the intention for the Highest Good. Others are standing ready at home for all comers to inquire about the good life provided by the Highest Good. Thus some were travelers and others receptionists for visitors.

You, as a Great One, made me proud one day in ancient Egypt. As the sun came out from behind a cloud, you listened intently to me. Then, stretching your right arm up to the clouds, you contacted the Arcturians asking about who they were. You learned that they are the ancestors – those who have come and gone from human and physical lifetimes – and that they are either resting before going forward on a mission or making plans to do so. In essence you did your first sojourn reading of your own lifetime, drawing from the memories of the ancestors, the agreements that you made before incarnation that would determine your life.

Since that time, you have developed a great understanding about the nature of a lifetime as being all about love. You know that beginning a new lifetime is a sincere event, one in which there is no possibility of demise of any kind because none was planned. However, if one does wish to wholly engage in the process of loving love, one consciously chooses love in both having love and lacking love. When one chooses to do this, one often has great reversals, moving from having love to lacking love and back again, but never falters about what life is all about.

When great choices for love meet in one lifetime, there is indeed the fullness of the understanding and willingness to participate in love. It is an expression of willingness to enjoy being in love and to seek to return love, all in the same lifetime. It seems contradictory, but one is not consistently at peace with one or the other until one finally comes to realize that just one element is responsible for both experiences. That one element is me, the Peaceful One, your ever present and reliable local resource for infinite love. Therefore, the reversal experiences are mainly for the integration of the Conscious Mind, as the Higher Mind is blissfully aware of itself as love.

As one lapses into retro vision of a past experience of either lack or presence of love, one sees both as a desire for the same thing. With the sure knowledge that one's Peaceful One is always at the controls of the situation, one knows were to turn. Mostly, one merely works through the grief situations in peace and moves on knowing that all experiences can only be benign and nothing else. Should one despair of ever finding true love again after having lost it, one should reflect that the love of one's Peaceful One is available all of the time simply by requesting it. Should one despair of ever finding true love, having never experienced it, then one should reflect that once one has no fear of being alone or abused, that nothing really matters, for the Peaceful One must be benign in all cases. Thus the fullness of love must be on the way.

Where one really gets upset is when the Conscious Mind enters the game and begins to name the state of non-love consciousness as despicable, miserable, well-deserved, etc. In these cases, the self-naming should be recognized as a fiction created by the smaller, less competent mind trying to command a situation of which it has no understanding. Nevertheless, when one mind ceases to function as a leader and the other takes over, there is a transference of emotional energy the likes of which cannot be explained.

For when one moves from fear to trust in the Higher Mind, then one can experience joy and the expectation of more and better to come. When one moves from joy to fear, then one looses all hope of ever being happy and despair ensues. Thus the act of changing minds is the proverbial changing of fortunes.

Even one small act of true love blows the cover, so to speak, on the definition of being unloved. Provided that the ego is not allowed to enter and dismiss the evidence of love as dubious, then the entrance of joy is opened. We recommend that every small evidence of love, whatever its source, be honored for what it is.

Thus we come once again to the eternally helpful and enviously effective method of handling both situations at one time. Making the infinity sign in front of the individual who is thinking of a false self-definition forbids the ego from interfering. The infinity sign does not have a place for doubt, as the center is closed. Thus we assert the need to be about using the infinity sign whenever there is doubt.

Joyce: That sounds like a wonderful idea. It is so easy and effective. What else would you suggest?

Peaceful One: Take every small opportunity to do something you love out of love. To do so belies all grief, especially if it is tangible. Thus, you often go about making a dress for one that you love such as your granddaughter. Then you can see that you are a good sewer and that the dress will be as well-loved as well as the dressmaker. It is a good way to keep doubt on the run. Both the act of making the dress and the love coming as a result of giving it are honored. Thus we think of the days' activities as being productive if they are about making something for love. As one just lets one beloved event flow to the next then one loves love and thus it will be their experience to be loved.

A popular phrase is *"be the love that one wants to have"* and it is a good one. But a better explanation also adds the understanding that doing so is not just a mimicry performed for a result. It should be the process of love creating a new mental and emotional universe for oneself. In short, one is investing in one's own personal universe of love as a warm and benign place in which to exist. It heals, prospers, and attracts all others interested in the same thing.

Therefore, one does not apply for love before it is given. One makes love happen by being love in motion. All love counts, even the little moments of enjoying a day of grace.

Joyce: This is very helpful. It is like saying that messing around with love is a good way to brew up some love. One thought, however, comes to mind. You said that one's Peaceful One is in control of our experiences of love or non-love, but this last discussion implies that the Conscious Mind is an essential participant. Would you explain that better?

Peaceful One: When one comes for love in the everyday kind of way of just doing what one loves to do with love in their heart, contentment expands and creates more and more experiences of happiness. Indeed, the

114

Conscious Mind, destined to develop into a grand lover, needs the experience of constantly choosing to love and to enjoy each moment of it. It is the same reason that no one can love without being loved in return.

God created the universe out of love, for love, and with love. When love is chosen, the light bulb is plugged into the universal love socket and the power starts to flow. God literally says: "*Let there be light.*" When love is not chosen, the power does not flow and karma must remind one over and over again of the consequences of the non-love choice. By making choice after choice, the will to love is exercised and the Conscious Mind emerges as a really good lover. It learns the state of non-love as well as the state of love, and never chooses the former ever again. Thus the world ends much like it started in the Garden of Eden with the choice to know and to choose God or not. The difference this time is that the not-to-love option is never again a viable one.

Thus the world, which was designed to develop and nurture the Conscious Mind, could be closed for business and left to be a beautiful park of remembrance for a time when suffering could be chosen for its own sake, but in the end was forsaken.

Joyce: So are you saying that when this all comes to pass, that Conscious Minds born to be able to fear, become great lovers by choosing to love?

Peaceful One: That is so. They will have all graduated into being fine and loving beings of much use to the Divine Creator for the accomplishment of great feats of love everywhere.

Joyce: So you are saying that the Earth is sort of a nursery school for Conscious Minds. Well that explains the mess that we've made of the Earth and the need for so much soul guidance, thank you very much. I vote we graduate them all and do something different.

Peaceful One: Would that be because you are tired of cleaning up the messes that little ones make or because you are proud of the progress that has been made as the advanced classes are filled with adept students planning on great careers?

Joyce: I guess a little of both. Sometimes, I just want to move on to better experiences and skip the painful ones.

Peaceful One: How about the need to give the teacher a rest break and to allow the children to go out in the play yard and burn up some energy on their own? Call them in only when they are ready to learn some more of what will save them making much trouble in the play yard. And how about your farm serve as a retreat for that rest break and the trips to the cities and places of work serve as classrooms? How nice to have both.

Joyce: It is amazing how you can pack so much insight into a few analogies. You are a great teacher and I want to be like you. When I show up to do classes, I just channel you and do my best and then leave. The people find their own Peaceful One. That's about all that I can do. Besides, I have my own life plan to manifest by doing all of this that I love with love. So how am I doing and what grade would you give me?

Peaceful One: I would grade you with the love and friendship of many. So the question is: *How close is close when nearer is dearer?* Yes, my dear, there are many approaching at warp speed to be at your side, so do not delay applying all of these little lessons and do apply for your graduation certificate for it is just about time for the commencement ceremonies to begin.

Joyce: Thanks. I really don't feel the panic about being alone anymore. It seems that I have enough contentment these days to be relaxed and alert, but not angry or resentful. That's as much a sign of progress for me as any, for I well know the difference between peace and grief. Time does heal all wounds, but talking with one's Peaceful One is the active healing ingredient in time. One's Peaceful One is one's local source for the infinite love of the universe and it delivers as much as one can consume while ordering up more and more. Sweet!

Peaceful One: In writing this book, you have so opened a new way for all to understand and to use the emotional highway created by peacefulness. Now we would like to commission another device for building the bridge between dimensions called: *The Peacemakers Circle.*

As you add resources to your classes and website, they will attract all who want to use the doorway to all good things and educate themselves on all of the little ways that the Conscious Mind avoids such a fine thing. Your work will offer much advice, success stories, and even more advanced information. For as people come and discover their own unique talents, their efforts will provide a way for so much more good that none in their right mind will want a day to pass without checking the website to see what new insights are available or rereading a chapter of your books to find a favorite quote.

Joyce: I hope that my work will serve the needs of people all over the world to know their own Peaceful One and to ask for the resources that they need to be healthy and happy. With all of that going on, there will be much more peace on the Earth. And with peace, there will be the joy of being alive and sharing one's gifts with others. It will truly be a Highest Good place to be.

Peaceful One: Well, then, my dearest one, we have nearly completed this book and once again look forward to the next. Do you think that it will ever end? Do you think that I will ever run out of wisdom or love to give you? Do you think that all who come will get enough to startle them into attention and want the same? Would it be possible that all who have come to read this book will want to walk through the same doorway as you and meet even more of the residents of this peaceful cave of consciousness? You have, after all only met a very few. There are crowds of them waiting for you to be healthy and wise enough to be able to speak to them.

Well, my dear, we will leave that up to Dear Readers everywhere to answer, for all are made whole who say that they want to be. All are cured and healed, who want to be. All are made prosperous who want to be. And that is the end of this story. I don't have anything more to say about that, as Forest Gump used to say.

Joyce: Forest Gump is the perfect example of one who had little intelligence and so had to trust others and his life plan, so I'd say that he is a good example of trusting

118

the Highest Good. Besides he learned a lot about life from a box of chocolates.

Peaceful One: When one is born, there is never a moment when one is not nourished, fortified, and directed by their Peaceful One. If no Conscious Mind fears and regrets enter into the mix, one's body is whole and healthy until the determined time to pass into another state of existence comes. Thus it is finally time to discuss the resurrection of the body from grief to wholeness. As the next book will be entitled: *A Diary of Rejuvenation,* we have much to say about how peace heals.

Joyce: What a tremendous topic that will be! Nearly everyone has grief about growing old and are you saying that you will tell us how to stay younger and live longer? I expect that this will get a lot of attention.

Peaceful One: How can one grow older when one is only the same age as the Peaceful One allows, which is always benign, beautiful, and wholly conscious of being loved? So the book will be more about how to get real about life forces and how to cooperate with them. Until then, I'll say *Godspeed*.

Joyce: And in a cloud of dust, we ask: "Who was that friend who brought us so much peace?" Thanks.

+

Dear Reader, will you join me in the next book and retire all thoughts that you might have about being sick or old and follow the wise and productive guidance that we are about to be given regarding the health and longevity of our bodies? After all, if we didn't have disease and aging to worry about, maybe we'd really be peaceful. As you know, when you have peace, you have everything. Just as in days gone by, there were always both the troublemakers and the peacemakers, but I call all of you to accompany me so that we can conquer all fear and be peacemakers for the rest of our lives. I give you peace!

Blessing for all Readers

Peace to all who came here looking for something good. Let them keep what they found close to their hearts and come again often to find much more. And with that we invite them to invite others who are experiencing the same tragedy of never having been introduced properly to the Maker of the Universe. We are here to help, as you apply much practice, patience and forgiveness of grief, until we can safely say to you: "You have arrived. You are in the Presence of God." Amen.

Resources

Once one has decided to seek the path of the Peacemakers, one needs to be able to explain to others how and why they have done so. Did you realize that while you were studying these books to find out how you could be healed and live in peace, you were being offered the gift of how to help all others who cross your path seeking the same? Thus we have revised The Long Story given in earlier books to include a much higher view of who we are, why we are here, and where we are going. Use it for your own inspiration and share it with all others who seek the path of peace.

The Long Story

When the Bible says that in the beginning there was God, it is referring to the time before time was created. God, knowing that love is all that there is, existed in peace and contentment, but wished for another to share the giving and receiving love. In that moment of desire to love another, souls were created just for the purpose of being in love with God, who is love itself. We are those souls designed to be loved and our true name is Beloved Ones.

These souls know that there is only love and only good, nothing else. Love is their being, for they were created out of love. They live and breathe love, and do nothing but love. Those souls – truly children of God – live lifetime after lifetime as humans with the time in between (called sojourns) devoted to reviewing the experience gained in the prior lifetime and planning more experiences of love in the next.

When we were created, we remained within the Body or Presence of God and never left. As souls, we know each other intimately and help and support each other through constant communication and assistance. All together, we are known as the Great Oneness.

In order for the souls to have the opportunity to have experiences and to propagate new souls, God created the physical universe with all of the stars, planets, and beings that live there. The physical universe and all beings living there are living within the Body of God. The souls entered into many experiences in the universe, first as spirit beings and then, later, as incarnated beings. The solar system of Earth, Venus, and Mars is the gift and responsibility of the Christ Consciousness who has a grand plan for peace for these places. He is ably assisted by the thirteen Guardians of the Earth – great spirit beings who have charge of peace on the planet Earth.

The physical universe consists of orbs of conscious energy working together to form complex living and material beings. Together they form physical experiences, which express God in various forms and expressions. These little orbs are all friendly, benign, and work in cooperation to maintain life. To be able to contact them, one needs to be friendly and to ask for assistance, which is their delight to give. Finally, one needs to be appreciative of their help.

All together these orbs cooperate with the souls choosing to enter into animal bodies perfected to be human. As humans, we have the gift of free will to choose to love or not to love. When a human is conceived, a projection of the Great Mind of the soul is sent to live in the human baby body. This mind is only a small portion of the greater soul mind and is essentially an offspring individuating into life experiences. Through these life experiences, the small mind (called the Conscious Mind) chooses love more and more faithfully, seeking to remember the Presence of God. The hallmark of the Presence of God is peace.

As humans, we are confused by the presence of the two minds – the Conscious Mind of the physical body and the Higher Mind of the soul – for a human has both to use. The Conscious Mind, starting with the prospect of being a separated individual, does not think that it is included within God, so it thinks thoughts of separation, fear, and anxiety. These fears and anxieties eventually give rise to the same beliefs within others. Over time, societies as a whole develop to support a grief mentality. All grief and harm is due to the experiences of the Conscious Minds living in fear. Therefore, bad things that happen are all functions of the Conscious Mind and its influence on society. Fear resides in the Conscious Mind and nowhere else, but it influences people to do bad things, thus giving rise to the belief and experience of evil.

Once one realizes that the world is designed or wired to be peaceful and that only one's Conscious Mind thinks otherwise, one is faced with the problem of gaining control of the fearful thinking and bringing both minds into cooperation for the same goal: The Highest Good. The Highest Good means good in all things and is ultimately defined as realizing that one is in the Presence of God. With a little self-discipline, the fearful thinking can be discouraged and trust in the Highest Good can grow. Eventually, fewer fearful events show up in one's life and one begins to heal their illness and anxiety. Eventually many more good events come to be, and trust in the good grows. This deep trust in the Highest Good manifests even more good.

The human body is surrounded by the energy field called the aura, which is where the soul feeds the body life energy through spirals of energy entering and exiting through the chakras. A chakra is a spinning vortex of energy either entering or leaving the body. If the chakra is spinning clockwise, there is incoming energy, if it is spinning counterclockwise there is energy and toxins being taken out. The body needs both vortexes to be healthy. If the chakras are closed with fear, grief, and anxiety, then neither the incoming energy nor the outgoing energy can function properly . The body is deprived of new life and filled with unreleased toxins, and is, thus, diseased. Removing fears through forgiveness is essentially how the body heals itself, as this act opens its chakras. If forgiveness is practiced consistently enough, the body stabilizes and rejuvenates itself daily. All is accomplished by the presence of the soul with its benign intentions for the success of the body and Conscious Mind.

When one opens to channel, one opens one's crown chakra to the Higher Mind of the soul, thus healing the body as well as making conscious contact with the Great Oneness of other souls. Once contact has been made, the Conscious Mind can ask for, and receive, benign and healing answers from the Higher Mind. This is where Edgar Cayce received his information in his readings. As was his experience, most of the inquiries are for healing, but also questions about the nature of the universe, how to live peacefully, and the prospect of a more peaceful Earth are all favorite topics of Higher Mind.

Once one decides to try to open one's chakras to contact with Higher Mind, one needs to relax one's body, take a few deep breaths and remain very peaceful. The form of address is a friendly one with the expectation that no harm will be done and much good will be given. The messages can come through as thoughts, feelings, images, or music. The more you practice, the better your contact gets and your chakras open wider and more reliably. The value of doing this is enormous. The ancient Egyptians who learned their math, geometry, science, and methods of constructing the pyramids from beings that they contacted through conversations with their Higher Minds can testify to that. Clearly contacting your Higher Mind is a healing and beneficial thing to do.

The Peace and Light Association is dedicated to educating the public about this type of information and hosts a website, publishes books, and arranges conferences. Our intention is that you enjoy the Highest Good and nothing else.

On our website, **PeaceandLight.net**, we have created a Peacemaker's library of short readings on many topics around the Higher Mind. In addition, announcements regarding the most recent publications will be posted. All books are available on Amazon.com. Just look for the author page of Joyce McCartney.

www.ingramcontent.com/pod-product-compliance
Lightning Source LLC
Chambersburg PA
CBHW071820090426
42737CB00012B/2147